高等学校英语专业规划教材

英语专业学术论文写作教程

文　斌　编著

华中科技大学出版社
中国·武汉

图书在版编目(CIP)数据

英语专业学术论文写作教程/文　斌　编著. —武汉：华中科技大学出版社，2010.12(2023.8重印)
　ISBN 978-7-5609-6564-2

　Ⅰ. 英…　Ⅱ. 文…　Ⅲ. 英语-论文-写作-高等学校-教材　Ⅳ. H315

中国版本图书馆 CIP 数据核字(2010)第 177177 号

英语专业学术论文写作教程

文　斌　编著

策划编辑：杨　鸥　刘　平	
责任编辑：定晓峰	
封面设计：刘　卉	
责任校对：李　琴	
责任监印：朱　玢	

出版发行：华中科技大学出版社(中国·武汉)　　电话：(027)81321913
　　　　　武汉市东湖新技术开发区华工科技园　　邮编：430223

印　　刷：广东虎彩云印刷有限公司
开　　本：787mm×1092mm　1/16
印　　张：10.25
字　　数：260 千字
版　　次：2023 年 8 月第 1 版第 12 次印刷
定　　价：38.00 元

本书若有印装质量问题，请向出版社营销中心调换
全国免费服务热线：400-6679-118　　竭诚为您服务
版权所有　侵权必究

前　　言

　　学术论文写作是英语专业学生的一门重要课程。本书主要是针对英语专业本科高年级学生和研究生编写的。本书主要围绕三条主线展开。这三条主线分别是本书题目中的三个关键词：学术、论文、写作。掌握基本的英语写作技巧是提高学术论文写作能力的基础，熟悉英语论文框架结构和写作步骤是提高英语学术论文写作能力的核心，而了解学术性写作特点是提高英语学术论文写作能力的必备条件。

　　本书的第一、二单元主要介绍了学术研究和学术论文的本质与特点。第三单元探讨了写作作为交际手段的基本要求。第四单元对学术性写作的七大特点进行了讨论。第五、六、七三个单元介绍了论文写作的基本步骤，如何列提纲和进行段落写作。第八到十一单元对摘要、引言、文献回顾、结语等学术论文的主要组成部分的写作方法进行了详细介绍。第十二到十七单元主要分析了如何将收集的资料进行加工整理并以正确的方式在论文中进行表述。第十八单元介绍了文中引用和参考文献的格式。

　　本书具有如下特点。

　　第一，学术论文是对学术研究内容的总结，是和其他研究工作者进行交流的手段。所以本书首先介绍的是学术研究的特点，以便读者能更清楚地了解学术论文的本质和特点。

　　第二，内容齐全，涵盖面广。包括论文写作的主要方面，如选题、材料收集及评估、提纲、段落写作、衔接与连贯、文献引用及其标注等。

　　第三，切合实际，针对性强。主要针对英语专业本科高年级学生和研究生编写。本书对论文写作的主要组成部分分单元进行了详细介绍，有利于学生理解和模仿。

　　第四，作者编写本书时考虑到了不同层次学生的水平和上课的实际学时，在安排本书内容时尽量做到内容丰富，重点突出，便于老师和学生根据实际需要对教材内容进行增补、删减或调整。本科生学习的重点可放在第二、五、六、七、八、九、十、十一、十八单元。而研究生则可有选择地对其他单元进行学习。

　　第五，本书配有大量的和论文写作有关的练习并提供了参考答案，便于老师进行教学，也便于学生自学。

　　由于作者水平有限，在编写过程中难免有漏误之处，欢迎使用本书的师生和其他读者批评指正。

编　者
2010 年 7 月

Contents

Unit 1 What is research? (1)
   1.1 Definition of research (1)
   1.2 Characteristics of research (1)
   1.3 Research process (2)

Unit 2 What is a research paper? (6)
   2.1 Definition of a research paper (6)
   2.2 The basic criteria of a research paper (6)
   2.3 Misconceptions to avoid (8)
   2.4 The importance of writing a research paper (8)
   2.5 Structure of a research paper (9)

Unit 3 Features of effective writing (13)
   3.1 Introduction (13)
   3.2 Purpose (13)
   3.3 Audience (13)
   3.4 Focus (14)
   3.5 Organization (14)
   3.6 Support and elaboration (14)
   3.7 Style (15)
   3.8 Conventions (16)

Unit 4 Features of academic writing (20)
   4.1 Introduction (20)
   4.2 Complexity (20)
   4.3 Formality (20)
   4.4 Objectivity (20)
   4.5 Explicitness (20)
   4.6 Hedging (21)
   4.7 Responsibility (21)

Unit 5 Steps in writing a research paper (27)
   5.1 Introduction (27)
   5.2 Selecting a research topic (27)
   5.3 Narrowing down the topic (27)
   5.4 Developing a research question (28)
   5.5 Finding sources (28)
   5.6 Evaluating sources (29)

5.7	Taking notes	(29)
5.8	Developing a research thesis	(30)
5.9	Creating an outline	(30)
5.10	Writing the first draft	(30)
5.11	Revision	(30)

Unit 6 Developing an outline .... (33)

6.1	Functions of an outline	(33)
6.2	Beginning an outline	(33)
6.3	Four features of an outline	(33)
6.4	Form of the outline	(35)
6.5	Two sample outline that illustrates many of the above-mentioned points	(36)

Unit 7 Writing academic paragraphs .... (39)

7.1	Topic sentences and their support in a paragraph	(39)
7.2	Building a paragraph	(39)
7.3	Incorporating sources within paragraphs	(40)
7.4	Different types of paragraphs in a research paper	(40)
7.5	Developing paragraphs	(41)

Unit 8 What is an abstract? .... (51)

8.1	Definition of an abstract	(51)
8.2	Functions of an abstract	(51)
8.3	Some misconceptions of an abstract	(51)
8.4	Abstracts and others types of summaries	(52)
8.5	Differences across disciplines	(52)
8.6	Major elements in an abstract	(52)
8.7	When to write the abstract	(53)
8.8	How to write an abstract	(53)

Unit 9 Introduction for a research paper .... (57)

9.1	What is the purpose of the introduction?	(57)
9.2	What questions will be answered in the introduction?	(57)
9.3	How research introductions are organized	(58)
9.4	Language used in the introduction	(60)
9.5	Summary	(61)

Unit 10 Writing a literature review .... (65)

10.1	What is a literature review?	(65)
10.2	Purpose	(65)
10.3	Reasons for writing a literature review	(65)
10.4	Questions a literature review should answer	(66)

10.5	Structure of a literature review	(67)
10.6	Steps in writing literature review	(67)
10.7	Examples	(69)

Unit 11 Conclusion (74)

11.1	What is a conclusion and what is its purpose?	(74)
11.2	What should you do when writing a conclusion?	(74)
11.3	Things to avoid in the conclusion	(75)
11.4	Sample conclusions	(75)

Unit 12 Summary (78)

12.1	Reasons for writing summaries	(78)
12.2	Definition of summary	(78)
12.3	Preparations	(78)
12.4	How to write summaries	(79)
12.5	How to include summaries in your text	(79)
12.6	Examples	(80)

Unit 13 How to paraphrase? (88)

13.1	What is paraphrase?	(88)
13.2	Why to paraphrase?	(88)
13.3	Length of paraphrases	(88)
13.4	How to paraphrase a source	(88)
13.5	Paraphrase or quote?	(89)
13.6	Examples	(90)

Unit 14 Expressing your voice in a research paper (94)

14.1	What is voice?	(94)
14.2	The features of voice in academic writing	(94)
14.3	Factors that influence the effective use of voice	(94)
14.4	Appropriate use of voice in academic writing	(95)
14.5	Editing and revising for voice	(96)

Unit 15 How to synthesizing information (98)

15.1	What is a synthesis?	(98)
15.2	Synthesis and your writing purpose	(98)
15.3	Two types of syntheses	(99)
15.4	Using synthesis in your writing	(99)
15.5	Examples of using synthesis in your writing	(100)

Unit 16 Reporting verbs (105)

16.1	Introduction	(105)
16.2	Different reporting verbs	(105)

16.3	Reporting verbs and your point of view	(106)
16.4	Reporting verbs and the author's point of view	(107)
16.5	Usage patterns of reporting verbs	(108)
16.6	Language points to be considered when using reporting verbs	(109)

Unit 17 Argument in research papers (112)

17.1	Introduction	(112)
17.2	What is an argument?	(112)
17.3	Evidence	(114)
17.4	Relationship between argument and evidence	(114)
17.5	Counterargument	(115)
17.6	The role of audience and language in argument	(115)
17.7	An example of argument in an essay	(116)

Unit 18 The Harvard style of referencing (119)

18.1	Introduction	(119)
18.2	Citing references in text using the Harvard system	(120)
18.3	Compiling the reference list and bibliography	(122)
18.4	Websites	(124)
18.5	The Harvard and APA referencing systems	(124)

Keys (129)

Bibliography (155)

Unit 1　What is research?

1.1　Definition of research

A research paper is to report what you have done in your research, so before we look at how to write a research paper, we need to investigate into the nature of research.

Generally speaking, research is the systematic process of collecting and analyzing information (data) in order to increase our understanding of the phenomenon which we are concerned with or interested in. In order to avoid some misconceptions of the nature of research, we should keep in mind that research is not mere information gathering, nor mere transportation of facts from one place to another.

1.2　Characteristics of research

Research is a process through which we attempt to achieve systematically and with the support of data the answer to a question, the solution to a problem, or a greater understanding of a phenomenon. This process has seven distinct characteristics.

1.2.1　Research originates with a question or problem

The world is filled with unanswered questions, unresolved problems. Everywhere we look, we observe things that cause us to ask questions. An inquisitive mind is the beginning of research.

Look around you. Consider the unresolved situations that evoke these questions: Why? What's the cause of that? What does it all mean? These are everyday questions. With questions like these, research begins.

1.2.2　Research requires a clear expression of a goal

A clear statement of the problem is of great importance. The statement asks the researcher, "What exactly do you intend to do?" This is basic and is required for the success of any research work. Without it, the research is on shaky ground.

1.2.3　Research requires a specific plan of procedure

Research is a search-and-discover task explicitly planned in advance. Researchers plan their overall research design and specific research methods in a purposeful way — that is, to yield data relevant to their particular research problem. Depending on the specific research question, different designs and methods will be more or less appropriate.

1.2.4　Research usually divides the principal problem into more manageable subproblems

The whole is composed of the sum of its parts. That is a universal natural law; that is also a good principle to follow in thinking about one's principal goal in research.

1.2.5　Research is guided by the specific research problem, question, or hypothesis

Having stated the problem and the subproblems, each subproblem is then viewed through a hypothesis. A hypothesis is a reasonable guess. It may direct your thinking to the possible source of information that will aid in resolving the research problem.

We must remember hypotheses are never proved nor disproved; they are either supported or not supported (rejected).

1.2.6　Research requires the collection and interpretation of data

Having now isolated the problem, divided it into subproblems, the next step is to collect data and to organize them in meaningful ways so that they can be interpreted.

Data, events, happenings, and observations are of themselves only data, events, happenings, and observations — nothing more. But all these are potentially meaningful. The significance of the data depends on the way the human brain extracts meaning from those data. In research, data unprocessed by the human brain are worthless.

Data demand interpretation. But no rule or no formula will lead the researcher precisely to the correct interpretation. Interpretation is subjective: It depends entirely on the logical mind, inductive reasoning skill, and objectivity of the researcher.

1.2.7　Research is, by its nature, cyclical

Research is never conclusive. In exploring an area, one comes across additional problems that need resolving. One research leads to another research. Every researcher soon learns that genuine research creates more problems than it resolves. Such is the nature of the discovery of knowledge.

1.3　Research process

1.3.1　Identify the research problem

You will most likely start doing research because you have a particular interest in a particular field. To find out more about this interest of yours, you must identify an approach that you will take in order to undertake this research. You may find, in thinking about your area further, that there is something which is not working, or which is unknown, or perhaps which is hypothesised, but that needs to be tested. This is the context for your research — your research problem. The next thing that you need to do is to turn that problem into a question or a statement — which you will use to address this problem.

1.3.2　Asking a research question

Your research question (or questions) should be your tool(s) for addressing the issue that you have identified as being of interest to you. The way you ask the question is vital to determining what kind of research you will conduct.

The question you ask will also generate a number of other questions, or subquestions. Things to bear in mind in forming questions to ask is to be realistic in what you can answer (with the time/resources you have available), and also in how many questions you are answering.

1.3.3 Doing literature review

Research cannot exist in a vacuum. In order to be scientific and exact, your research must itself be based within the context of "the literature" (i. e. books, journals, newspaper articles). Your research should show that you have read around both your subject and the methodologies that you have chosen — your questions, methodologies and methods will also largely be shaped or influenced by what you have read.

1.3.4 Identify methodologies and methods

There are a wide array of research methodologies and methods. Research methodologies can take the form of experiment, case study, and/or survey, can be either, or a mixture of, qualitative (based on words and meanings) or quantitative (based on statistics and their meanings), and can incorporate a variety methods to generate data (e. g. observations, questionnaires), as well as varieties of ways of analysing this data. The following are some common ways of designing a methodology that answers your research question(s), and methods of generating data.

1.3.4.1 Methodologies

Experiment: An experiment-based methodology is where, simply speaking, a stimulus is applied (e. g. a new system of teaching science to primary school students) and its response is measured (e. g. by analysing exam results). Such a methodology is most often linked with a quantitative (i. e. statistical) approach, but this is not necessarily the case. To maximise the validity of such studies, there are usually some elements of controlling of/for variables (such as by having a group of students who are taught differently to normal, and another group who are taught the same as normal). It can be linked with methods such as observation, interview etc.

Survey: A survey is a study of a phenomenon over/within a geographic region. This could involve, say, a survey of the crime rates of every major city in a certain country, or a survey of a sample of bloggers' political motivations.

Case study: A case study, as the name implies, is a study of a specific "case", or group of "cases" — a "case" being an individual person, an organisation, a school etc. Some research will focus on one single case and attempt to generate "rich" data; and some research will focus on a number of cases, either which are significantly different from one another, or which are similar, or which are clustered or spread in a geographic/ socio-political spread. Focussing on a number of cases can approach a survey design — or sometimes large-scale surveys can be used in order to identify specific cases which might be of interest to the researcher.

In order to address a complex question, you will need to identify what methodologies and methods — or, more likely, combinations of methodologies and methods — are most likely to address your particular question to your satisfaction.

1.3.4.2 Methods

Research methods can be various, the following are the most frequently used.

Questionnaires: Sometimes a questionnaire can contain a number of questions with a number of options to choose from (i.e. where you have to "tick a box, or number of boxes"). Other questionnaires may be questions with space in which to write more free-form or detailed answers. Some questionnaires will have a mixture of both types of questions. Both types of questions can have their strengths and weaknesses.

Observations: Observation is paying close attention to an environment, its context, and its social dynamics. It can be systematic (where the researcher will be recording, for example, how many times a person scratches his/her head), or more free-form where the researcher watches everything and records as much detail as they can or that they feel is appropriate.

Interviews: Interviews can be between one person and another, or in a group setting. They can be "structured" (where the interviewer will ask a predetermined set of questions), "semi-structured" (where the interviewer will ask a number of questions based on an outline of topics to be covered), or "unstructured" (where the interviewer will ask questions based on whatever emerges during the interview itself — or, often, will not seem to ask questions, but rather facilitate or participate in a conversation).

Eliciting: Eliciting is a way of getting people to talk about something, based on a prompt, such as a photograph, or piece of music. For example, in research done with young children, an interview might be intimidating, but a photograph (for example) gives the child or children something to talk about, while giving the researcher an opportunity to observe reactions to the photograph.

1.3.5 Analysis

Once you have collected your data (e.g. filled-in questionnaires, interviews recorded and transcribed), you must now do something with it! Your data is of no use to anyone else if it is not interpreted.

1.3.6 Writing

Writing up your research into a report, paper, essay or thesis.

Exercise 1

Answer the following questions.

1. What is research?

2. What are the features of research?
3. What do we mean by the statement "research is cyclical"?
4. What methods do we often use in doing research?

Exercise 2

Study the following situation carefully and then write down as many reasonable guesses as possible to explain what has happened. A sample guess is offered.

You come home after dark, open the front door, and reach inside to turn on the lamp that stands on a nearby table. Your fingers find the switch. You turn it. No light.

In this situation what reasonable guesses — hypotheses — can you offer for the cause of the lamp failure?

A sample guess: The bulb has burned out.

Unit 2 What is a research paper?

2.1 Definition of a research paper

Many people are likely to associate a research paper with working with piles of books, and searching for other people's ideas. Yet a research paper is more than the sum of your sources, more than a collection of different pieces of information about a topic, and more than a review of the literature in a field. A research paper analyzes a perspective or argues a point. A research paper should present your own thinking backed up by others' ideas and information.

A research paper is a general term. It may be a term paper for a university course, a published article in an academic journal, or a thesis or a dissertation for a university degree. In this book, a research paper will be defined as **a documented report that focuses on an academic topic, and it is intended to inform the audience of the research topic, purpose, method, results, findings, conclusions, and recommendations.**

Then what factors will determine the nature of a research paper? From the term itself we can conclude that it should have two distinctive features. First it is the report of your research, thus should reflect the nature of research: identifying problems, asking questions, reading for other people's ideas, designing methodologies to work out the answers to the questions, and discussing the results of your findings.

Second, a research paper is a piece of academic writing, therefore, it should follow the rules for academic writing. For example, the topic should be well-chosen, the central idea clearly stated, the argument sufficiently supported and the sources acknowledged and properly documented.

2.2 The basic criteria of a research paper

There are some basic criteria that make up a research paper:

A research paper is a piece of academic writing. It has some definite requirements to be completed. First of all, a research paper has to have a precise and clear topic, which is related with some academic science. Secondly, a research paper has to be structured according to the academic requirements. It means that the first part of the research paper has to introduce the readers into the topic of the paper and present the research's background. The second part of the paper should explain the methods of research and describe the research process. The last part should sum up and conclude the research. It is also necessary to mention all the additional sources which were used as the research's background.

A research paper is argumentative in nature. Therefore you need to support your stand on an issue and use information as evidence to support your point, much as a lawyer uses evidence to make his case.

A research paper is an argument in which different parts are logically related and all centre around research questions. It is neither a simple recording of what has been done in your research nor a description of what has been found in your study. Writing a research paper involves more than just searching for information from books, articles, internet, artwork or people. It involves your thinking ability and your intellectual skills.

A research paper is based on logical arguments and findings. If you are doing an empirical research you must defend your arguments in terms of a sound model, a methodology to test that model, and findings which either do or do not support your model. If you are doing conceptual research, you must defend your arguments in terms of applying logic to explain the weaknesses or limitations you found in the previous research, either through a model or a well-structured narrative.

A research paper is based on your exploration of other people's ideas, rather than simply an analysis of your own thoughts. A research paper is finding out and interpreting the ideas of other people in the relevant field. This process is often referred to as literature review. When you write a research paper you build upon what you know about the subject and make a deliberate attempt to find out what experts know. A research paper involves surveying a field of knowledge in order to find the best possible information in that field.

As soon as you decide on the research paper topic you need to start working on the literature review. The collected information should then be summarized and paraphrased. Review of literature helps to evaluate the extent of your knowledge and understanding of the large amount of data available in your field.

Writing a research paper also includes synthesis and analysis. First you have to synthesize information from several sources. Then the information that you have gathered needs to be separated into its component parts and each part has to be analyzed and restructured. Then you will have to give your thoughts on each of these parts.

A research paper expresses the author's understanding of the topic based on experiments, facts, data and analyses. It should show your originality. The paper that results from your personal processes of evaluation, study, and synthesis will be a totally new creation. Although it is true that you use several and varied sources, your originality will be evident in your carefully crafted research paper.

While writing a research paper, you do not concentrate on just the literature review but also your own opinions and thoughts on the research paper topic. Whatever be the research paper topic, you need to do your own thinking and back it up with ideas and information that you have collected from other sources.

A research paper should provide its writer and its reader with new knowledge and a new understanding of a specific topic. The success of your research paper depends primarily on your critical judgment in selecting sources and on the originality and thoughtfulness of your treatment of the topic.

A research paper is properly and systematically documented. All the sources used need to be acknowledged. To prevent a reader from believing that the intellectual property of somebody else is, instead, yours, the words, ideas, and visuals of others must be recognized and documented. Thus, even though your research paper is a new and original work, none of it would have been possible without the various sources you consulted to prepare it.

2.3 Misconceptions to avoid

A research paper is not simply a generalized discussion of an issue. It should have a thesis — a clear point of view.

A summary of a source material, such as a book or an article, is not a research paper. There are two reasons that a summary doesn't fit with the definition of a research paper. First, a single source does not allow you to choose materials or to exercise your own judgment. Second, the organization cannot be your own since a summary has to follow the structure of the original source.

Repeating the ideas of others uncritically does not make a research paper. The research paper, by definition, has to reflect something about yourself. This could be an interpretation, a synthesis, or some other personal involvement.

Unproven personal opinion does not make a research paper. Despite the expectation to put some personal thinking into a research paper, you must have reasons for your beliefs and make them evident to readers. This means that even though individual thoughts and attitudes are important in some types of writing assignments, the research paper is not usually one of them. The exception to this is if you can support your ideas and attitudes.

To sum up we can say:

(1) A research paper is not "about" a subject.

(2) A research paper is not a summary of an article or a book (or other source material).

(3) A research paper is not repeating the ideas of others uncritically.

(4) A research paper is not putting together a series of quotations.

(5) A research paper is not expressing unsupported personal opinions.

(6) A research paper is not copying or accepting another person's work without acknowledging it.

2.4 The importance of writing a research paper

Why is learning to write research papers so important? There are several reasons for this practice. The first one is very practical and self-obvious: in most universities, a research paper is a partial requirement to get a degree. Thus writing a good research paper provides you with a decent grade to pass the class and earn credit.

Secondly, the skills you practise in writing a research paper are crucial to academic success. If you attain these skills while preparing your research for your paper, most likely you will put these skills to use again and again in differing ways in and out of school.

These skills are used in decisions about job assignments and promotions. These same skills are also used by physicians, engineers, accountants, and teachers.

Thirdly, even if you never become a professional writer you will follow the same procedure for various future assignments. It is likely you will become a better reader, for, as you go through the process of preparing the research paper you will practise critical thinking.

Fourthly, academic research papers can reveal something that you did not suspect about yourself. And that is your talent in scholarly research. Most of the students possessing strong analytical skills are usually the last ones to find out about it. Academic research papers develop abilities to investigate, evaluate, and summarize. They also teach to look for important data and manage it.

Last but not the least, academic research papers open new horizons and offer a lot of new information you had no idea about before writing one. This might lead you to do more investigations to satisfy your curiosity.

2.5 Structure of a research paper

To create a good research paper it is very necessary to understand the research paper structure, also known as the research paper layout.

The basic research paper requirements are: title page, table of contents, abstract, introduction, body (literature review, materials and method, results, discussion), conclusion, list of references and appendix.

2.5.1 The "title" of the research paper

The title page of the research paper should serve as an overview of the most important practical information related to the paper. Most of the time, it includes the title, name of the author(s), date, name of department and school, and name of the supervisor. It is very necessary to ensure that the title of the research paper should clearly identify the content and the subject matter of the report.

2.5.2 The table of contents (optional in short papers)

The purpose of the table of contents is to give the reader an idea of the extent and the structure of the paper so that to provide a navigator for the reader. In a long research paper, a table of contents should go on a separate page titled TABLE OF CONTENTS. It should contain, with the page number, the title of each chapter or division, followed by the title of each important subdivision, the appendix, if the paper has it and the bibliography.

2.5.3 Abstract

The abstract section is a short summary of the entire work. It should include: the purpose of the study, a brief description of the work, results, including specific data, and important conclusions of research paper or questions.

2.5.4 The introduction

The introduction serves as an orientation for the readers of the paper. It generally includes the context for the research question, a clearly stated thesis statement, the hypotheses, definitions and the structure of the paper.

2.5.5 Literature review

This part will describe the study that you have conducted based on various sources and your agreement or disagreement with the authors on the particular subject matter.

2.5.6 The methodology

This normally describes the methods that were used to attain the final goal of the paper or rather to explain the procedure. You can include comments on and reasons for choice of method (e.g. interviews, questionnaires, empirical material, statistics).

2.5.7 Results and findings

This is used to describe the various results and findings.

2.5.8 Conclusion

This section should provide a clear answer to your research question and sum up of the new knowledge you have acquired. You may also describe interesting observations, new questions and future work here.

2.5.9 References or works cited

This section gives details of the books, articles and websites that have been referred to in the research paper. You should include all sources that have been referred to in the text, and only sources that have been referred to in the text.

2.5.10 Appendix (optional)

Appendix should only be used if necessary. You may put here materials that are important to the reader, but not appropriate to be placed in the text itself, for example, tables, diagrams, and interview transcripts.

Exercise 1

Read the following extracts from a research paper and match them with the following headings:

Abstract   Introduction   Methods   Results   Discussion

1.
> This study reports on the sleep patterns of a boy with autism over the course of his fifth year of life. A one-year diary revealed seasonal changes in sleep patterns. The results are discussed in terms of their application to future research.

2.
> Parents often report sleep problems in children with autism (Callahan 1987; Rogers and Brown 1992). Moreover, research reveals that problems in sleep may be affected by seasonal changes (Robins, Williams, Jones, and Miller 1999). However, to date there have been no studies investigating the relationship between seasonal changes and sleep patterns in children with autism. Therefore, the purpose of the present study was to examine whether the sleep patterns of a child with autism were affected by seasonal changes.

3.
> The subject was a male with autism. His mother kept a diary of his sleep habits over the course of his fifth year of life, beginning on his fourth birthday and ending on his fifth birthday. Based on daily entries made in the diary, a trained researcher noted days indicating sleep problems (such as restlessness or wakefulness).

4.
> A total score was calculated for incidents of sleep problems. For each month, a score for sleep problems was determined by calculating the number of days in each month when these problems were recorded and summing the number across the three months for each season. The sleep problem scores for each of the three month seasons are presented in Table 1. As shown in both Table 1 and Figure 1, sleep problems increased in the fall and winter and decreased in the spring and summer.

5.
> This study reported on a seasonal pattern of sleep problems in a boy with autism during his fifth year of life. Specifically, the study found that disturbances in sleep problems occurred at higher frequencies in the winter and spring, and diminished during the summer and fall. It may be that seasonal changes in light cause these disturbances. In this study, sleep problems occurred during the seasons when the days are shortest and there is the least daylight in the northern hemisphere. In support of this assumption, previous research has found an increase in disturbances in behavior in children with developmental disabilities during the winter and fall (Marks, Cohen, and Winthrop 1991; Price 1995). Thus, future research is needed to determine if this seasonal pattern in sleep disturbance is found in other children with autism.

Exercise 2

Read a research paper you can find and try to answer as many of the following questions as possible.

1. What has previous research found about the topic?
2. How will this study add to the previous research?
3. What are the study's research questions and hypotheses?
4. What type of study?
5. Where was the research conducted?
6. How many subjects were in the study?
7. What were the characteristics of the subjects?
8. What were the inclusion and exclusion criteria for subject selection?
9. How were the subjects assigned to groups?
10. How was the study conducted?
11. What kinds of data were collected?
12. Are the instruments used valid?
13. Have other researchers used the instruments?
14. What are the findings?
15. Are the findings statistically significant?
16. How do the authors summarize the findings?
17. How do the authors interpret the findings?
18. What are the limitations of the study?
19. How do you interpret the findings?
20. Are the findings applicable to other people and settings?

Unit 3 Features of effective writing

3.1 Introduction

A research paper is a type of academic writing. Therefore to write a good research paper we have to learn something about the features of academic writing and effective writing. Effective writing is writing which has a logical flow of ideas and is cohesive. This means it holds together well because there are links between sentences and paragraphs. Writing which is cohesive works as a unified whole and is easy to follow because it uses language effectively to maintain a focus and to keep the reader "on track".

Effective writing has many features. The most important ones are **purpose**, **audience**, **focus**, **organization**, **support and elaboration**, **style**, and **conventions.**

3.2 Purpose

When we communicate with other people, we are usually guided by some purpose, goal, or aim. We may want to **express** our feelings. We may want simply to **explore** an idea or perhaps **entertain** or amuse our listeners or readers. We may wish to **inform** people or **explain** an idea. We may wish to **argue** for or against an idea in order to **persuade** others to believe or act in a certain way. We make special kinds of arguments when we are **evaluating** or **problem solving**. Finally, we may wish to **mediate** or negotiate a solution in a tense or difficult situation.

Focusing on your purpose as you begin writing helps you know what form to choose, how to focus and organize your writing, what kinds of evidence to cite, how formal or informal your style should be, and how much you should write.

3.3 Audience

Writing is a form of communication, and communication is almost always directed at an audience. An awareness of your audience is critical in determining your approach to the other of good writing.

An audience is a group of readers who reads a particular piece of writing. As a writer, you should anticipate the needs or expectations of your audience in order to convey information or argue for a particular claim. Your audience might be your instructor, classmates, the president of an organization, the staff of a management company, or any other number of possibilities. You need to know your audience before you start writing.

Once you know your audience, you are ready to begin writing. Knowing your audience enables you to select or reject details for that specific audience. In addition, different audiences expect different types or formats for texts. Mothers getting letters from children don't want to read a laboratory report about the events of the past month.

Knowing the knowledge level of your audience will help you determine how to write, how much information to include, how long to make your text, how subjective or objective you should be, and how formal or informal your text should be.

Knowing your audience helps you to make decisions about what information you should include, how you should arrange that information, and what kind of supporting details will be necessary for the reader to understand what you are presenting. It also influences the tone and structure of the document. In order to develop and present an effective argument, you need to be able to appeal to and address your audience.

3.4 Focus

Just as a photographer needs to focus on a particular subject to produce a clear picture, a writer needs to focus on a single topic or main idea in order to produce an effective piece of writing. An effective piece of writing establishes a single focus and sustains that focus throughout the piece.

By establishing a clear focus before we start to write, we can craft our writing into a coherent, unified whole. Finding a focus helps us find the significance in our writing, the message we want to convey to the audience, our reason for writing.

Establishing a clear focus also helps readers understand the point of the piece of writing. Readers don't want to read a paper filled with unrelated ideas; they read to learn something new, to be surprised, to gain a new insight on an old idea, to view something from a new perspective or angle.

Focus is also the critical feature that drives all the other features. Focus determines what choices the writer makes about everything from organizational structure to elaborative details to word choice, sentence length, and punctuation. At the same time, effective writers take advantage of the appropriate supporting features to strengthen the focus of their writing.

3.5 Organization

Organization is important to effective writing because it provides readers with a framework to help them fulfill their expectations for the text. A well-organized piece of writing supports readers by making it easy for them to follow, while a poorly organized piece leads readers through a maze of confusion and confounded or unmet expectations.

Organization, simply put, is the logical progression and completeness of ideas in a text. Instruction in organization focuses on two areas: the **text structures** specific to the particular genre and the **cohesive elements** that tie clauses, sentences, and paragraphs together into a cohesive whole.

3.6 Support and elaboration

Support and elaboration consists of the specific details and information writers use to develop their topic. The key to developing support and elaboration is getting *specific*. Good writers use concrete, specific details, and relevant information to construct mental images for their readers. Without this attention to detail, readers struggle to picture what the writer is talking about, and will often give up altogether.

Two important concepts in support and elaboration are *sufficiency and relatedness.*

Sufficiency refers to the amount of detail. Good writers supply their readers with sufficient details to comprehend what they have written. In narrative writing, this means providing enough descriptive details for the reader to construct a picture of the story in their mind. In expository writing, this means not only finding enough information to support your purpose, whether it is to inform or persuade your audience, but also finding information that is credible and accurate.

Sufficiency, however, is not enough. The power of your information is determined less by the quantity of details than by their *quality.*

Relatedness refers to the quality of the details and their relevance to the topic. Good writers select only the details that will support their focus, deleting irrelevant information. In narrative writing, details should be included only if they are concrete, specific details that contribute to, rather than detract from, the picture provided by the narrative. In expository writing, information should be included only if it is relevant to the writer's goal and strengthens rather than weakens the writer's ability to meet that goal.

3.7 Style

A writer's style is what sets his or her writing apart and makes it unique. Style is the way writing is dressed up to fit the specific context, purpose, or audience. Word choice, sentence fluency, and the writer's voice — all contribute to the style of a piece of writing. How a writer chooses words and structures sentences to achieve a certain effect is also an element of style.

Style is not a matter of right and wrong but of what is appropriate for a particular setting and audience. Consider the following two passages, which were written by the same author on the same topic with the same main idea, yet have very different styles:

"Experiments show that Heliconius butterflies are less likely to oviposit on host plants that possess eggs or egg-like structures. These egg mimics are an unambiguous example of a plant trait evolved in response to a host-restricted group of insect herbivores."

"Heliconius butterflies lay their eggs on Passiflora vines. In defense the vines seem to have evolved fake eggs that make it look to the butterflies as if eggs have already been laid on them."

What changed was the *audience.* The first passage was written for a professional journal read by other biologists, so the style is authoritative and impersonal, using technical terminology suited to a professional audience. The second passage, written for a popular science magazine, uses a more dramatic style, setting up a conflict between the butterflies and the vines, and using familiar words to help readers from non-scientific backgrounds visualize the scientific concept being described. Each style is appropriate for the particular audience.

3.8 Conventions

Conventions are the surface features of writing — mechanics, usage, and sentence formation. Conventions are a courtesy to the reader, making writing easier to read by putting it in a form that the reader expects and is comfortable with.

Mechanics are the conventions of print that do not exist in oral language, including spelling, punctuation, capitalization, and paragraphs.

Usage refers to conventions of both written and spoken language that include word order, verb tense, and subject-verb agreement.

Sentence formation refers to the structure of sentences, the way that phrases and clauses are used to form simple and complex sentences.

Exercise 1

Match the less formal expressions on the right with the more formal ones on the left.

1. I am writing
2. such a large number of
3. I find it difficult to believe that
4. express my disagreement
5. is seriously under-funded
6. inaccurate
7. a significant percentage
8. it is a well-known fact
9. opportunity
10. entitled

A. I thought I'd drop you a line
B. it can't be right that
C. so many
D. doesn't have enough money
E. wrong
F. chance
G. a lot of people
H. everyone knows
I. say how much I disagree
J. which was called

Exercise 2

What is the main purpose of the following passage?

A. To inform people about the relationship between eggs and cholesterol.
B. To convince people to eat "designer" eggs and egg substitutes.
C. To persuade people that eggs are unhealthy and should not be eaten.
D. To introduce the idea that dietary fat increases the blood cholesterol level.

Although they are an inexpensive supplier of vitamins, minerals, and high-quality protein, eggs also contain a high level of blood cholesterol, one of the major causes of heart disease. One egg yolk, in fact, contains a little more than two-thirds of the suggested daily cholesterol limit. This knowledge has caused egg sales to plummet in recent years, which in turn has brought about the development of several alternatives to eating regular eggs. One alternative is to eat substitute eggs. These egg substitutes are not really eggs, but they look somewhat like eggs when they are cooked. They have the advantage of having lower cholesterol rates, and they can be scrambled or used in baking. One disadvantage, however, is that they are not good for frying, poaching, or boiling. A second alternative to regular eggs is a new type of egg, sometimes called "designer" eggs. These eggs are produced by hens that are fed low-fat diets consisting of ingredients such as canola oil, flax, and rice bran. In spite of their diets, however, these hens produce eggs that contain the same amount of cholesterol as regular eggs. Yet, the producers of these eggs claim that eating their eggs will not raise the blood cholesterol in humans.

Egg producers claim that their product has been portrayed unfairly. They cite scientific studies to back up their claim. And, in fact, studies on the relationship between eggs and human cholesterol levels have brought mixed results. It may be that it is not the type of egg that is the main determinant of cholesterol but the person who is eating the eggs. Some people may be more sensitive to cholesterol derived from food than other people. In fact, there is evidence that certain dietary fats stimulate the body's production of blood cholesterol. Consequently, while it still makes sense to limit one's intake of eggs, even designer eggs, it seems that doing this without regulating dietary fat will probably not help reduce the blood cholesterol level.

Exercise 3

Who is the author's intended audience in the following passage ?

As more women in the United States move up the professional ladder, more are finding it necessary to make business trips alone. Since this is new for many, some tips are certainly in order. If you are married, it is a good idea to encourage your husband and children to learn to cook a few simple meals while you are away. They will be much happier and probably they will enjoy the experience. If you will be eating alone a good deal, choose good restaurants. In the end, they will be much better for your digestion. You may also find it useful to call the restaurant in advance and state that you will be eating alone. You will probably get better service and almost certainly a better table. Finally, and most importantly, anticipate your travel needs as a businesswoman; this starts with lightweight luggage which you can easily manage even when fully packed. Take a folding case inside your suitcase; it will come in extremely handy for dirty clothes, as well as for business documents and papers you no longer need on the trip. And make sure you have a briefcase so that you can keep currently required papers separate. Obviously, experience helps, but you can make things easier on yourself from the first by careful planning, so that right from the start you really can have a good trip!

Exercise 4

Read the following passages and write for each passage a topic sentence.
Passage 1

Any attempt to trace the development from the noises that babies make to their first spoken words leads to considerable difficulties. It is agreed that they enjoy making noises, and that during the first few months one or two noises sort themselves out as particularly indicative of delight, distress, sociability, and so on. But since these cannot be said to show the baby's intention to communicate, they can hardly be regarded as early forms of language. It is agreed, too, that from about three months they play with sounds for enjoyment, and that by six months they are able to add new sounds to their store. This self-imitation leads to deliberate imitation of sounds made or words spoken to them by other people. The problem then arisen so to the point at which one can say that these imitations can be considered as speech.

Passage 2

Before transplanting, check to see if the tree roots are moist; if they are not, soak them in water for two or more hours until they appear soggy. While the roots are soaking, find a sunny spot in which to plant the tree. The soil should be a dark brown color-indicating that it is rich in nutrients. If the soil is in poor condition, mix in peat moss or potting soil. Next, dig a hole big enough to allow the tree roots room to spread out. Place the tree in the hole and, while holding the tree straight, fill in the hole with dirt; pack the dirt lightly. Water the tree every day for a week so that the roots can take hold in the ground.

Exercise 5

Finish the incomplete paragraphs below by providing the missing idea.

Passage 1

Automatic cash machines are now a common sight in high streets all over Britain, and there is no doubt that they are a convenient way of withdrawing cash 24 hours a day and seven days a week. Customers have a plastic card and a four-figure personal identification number (PIN). When they put the card into the machine and type their PIN into the computer, customers can withdraw cash, check their bank balance, and sometimes even order a new cheque book and deposit money. A recent report from the National Consumer Council, however, has found (**missing idea**)_____. Customers have complained that they have not received the correct money, or that their bank statements show two debits for a single withdrawal. There have even been a few cases where customers say that their statements show a cash withdrawal, when they have never even used the machine.

Passage 2

As more women in the United States move up the professional ladder, more are finding it necessary to make business trips alone. Since this is new for many, (**missing idea**)_____. If you are married, it is a good idea to encourage your husband and children to learn to cook a few simple meals while you are away. They will be much happier and probably they will enjoy the experience. If you will be eating alone a good deal, choose good restaurant. You may also find it useful to call the restaurant in advance and state that you will be eating alone. You will probably get better service and almost certainly a better table. Finally, and most importantly, anticipate your travel needs as a business woman; this starts with light-weight luggage which you can easily manage even when fully packed. And make sure you have a briefcase so that you can keep currently required papers separate.

Unit 4　Features of academic writing

4.1　Introduction

Academic writing is in the standard written form of the language. It has one central point or theme with every part contributing to the major argument, without digressions or repetitions. Its objective is to inform rather than entertain. There are six main features of academic writing that are often discussed. Academic writing is to some extent: complex, formal, objective, explicit, hedged, and responsible.

4.2　Complexity

Written language is grammatically more complex than spoken language. It has more subordinate clauses, more "that/to" complement clauses, more long sequences of prepositional phrases, more attributive adjectives and more passives than spoken language.

Written texts are shorter and have longer, more complex words and phrases. They have more nominalisations, more noun based phrases, and more lexical variation. Written texts are lexically dense compared to spoken language — they have proportionately more lexical words than grammatical words.

4.3　Formality

In general this means in academic writing you should avoid:
A. colloquial words and expressions: "stuff", "a lot of", "thing", "sort of";
B. abbreviated forms: "can't", "doesn't", "shouldn't";
C. two word verbs: "put off", "bring up".

4.4　Objectivity

This means that the main emphasis should be on the information that you want to give and the arguments you want to make, rather than you. This is related to the basic nature of academic study and academic writing, in particular. Nobody really wants to know what you "think" or "believe". They want to know what you have studied and learned and how this has led you to your various conclusions. The thoughts and beliefs should be based on your lectures, reading, discussion and research and it is important to make this clear.

In general, avoid words like "I", "me", "myself". A reader will normally assume that any idea not referenced is your own. It is therefore unnecessary to make this explicit.

4.5　Explicitness

Academic writing is explicit in several ways.
(1) It is explicit in its signposting of the organisation of the ideas in the text. As a

writer of academic English, it is your responsibility to make it clear to your reader how various parts of the text are related. These connections can be made explicit by the use of different signalling words.

For example, if you intend your sentence to give extra information, make it clear.

He is born into a family, he marries into a family, and he becomes the husband and father of his own family. In addition, he has a definite place of origin and more relatives than he knows what to do with, and he receives a rudimentary education at the Canadian Mission School.

(2) It is explicit in its acknowledgment of the sources of the ideas in the text.

If you know the source of the ideas you are presenting, acknowledge it.

4.6 Hedging

It is often believed that academic writing is factual, simply to convey facts and information. However it is now recognised that an important feature of academic writing is the concept of cautious language, often called "hedging" or "vague language". In other words, it is necessary to make decisions about your stance on a particular subject, or the strength of the claims you are making. Different subjects prefer to do this in different ways.

Language used in hedging:

1. Introductory verbs: e.g. seem, tend, look like, appear to be, think, believe, doubt, be sure, indicate, suggest
2. Certain lexical verbs: e.g. believe, assume, suggest
3. Certain modal verbs: e.g. will, must, would, may, might, could
4. Adverbs of frequency: e.g. often, sometimes, usually
5. Modal adverbs: e.g. certainly, definitely, clearly, probably, possibly, perhaps, conceivably
6. Modal adjectives: e.g. certain, definite, clear, probable, possible
7. Modal nouns: e.g. assumption, possibility, probability
8. That clauses: e.g. It could be the case that...
    e.g. It might be suggested that...
9. To-clause + adjective: e.g. It may be possible to obtain.
    e.g. It is useful to study.

4.7 Responsibility

In academic writing you are responsible for demonstrating an understanding of the source text. You must also be responsible for, and must be able to provide evidence and justification for, any claims you make.

This is done by paraphrasing and summarising what you read and acknowledging the source of this information or ideas by a system of citation. We are going to look at this in greater detail in the following chapters in this book.

Exercise 1

Identify the language used to show hedging in the following pairs of sentences, and discuss how the hedging language indicates the stance of the writer.

1. It may be said that the commitment to some of the social and economic concepts was less strong than it is now.

   The commitment to some of the social and economic concepts was less strong than it is now.

2. By analogy, it may be possible to walk from one point in hilly country to another by a path which is always level or uphill, and yet a straight line between the points would cross a valley.

   By analogy, one can walk from one point in hilly country to another by a path which is always level or uphill, and yet a straight line between the points would cross a valley.

3. Nowadays the urinary symptoms seem to be of a lesser order.

   Nowadays the urinary symptoms are of a lesser order.

Exercise 2

Compare these two paragraphs and discuss which one is more objective.

   The question of what constitutes "language proficiency" and the nature of its cross-lingual dimensions is also at the core of many hotly debated issues in the areas of bilingual education and second language pedagogy and testing. Researchers have suggested ways of making second language teaching and testing more "communicative" (e. g. , Canale and Swain, 1980; Oller, 1979b) on the grounds that a communicative approach better reflects the nature of language proficiency than one which emphasizes the acquisition of discrete language skills.

   We don't really know what language proficiency is but many people have talked about it for a long time. Some researchers have tried to find ways for us to make teaching and testing more communicative because that is how language works. I think that language is something we use for communicating, not an object for us to study and we remember that when we teach and test it.

Exercise 3

Match the formal phrases in the boxes on the right with the informal phrases on the left.

	Informal	Formal
1	Everybody must...	Goods can be ordered directly from...
2	In our daily lives we experience the influence of...	Goods cannot be seen or touched...
3	We simply/just order goods from...	It is essential/crucial/vital that all parties...
4	Let us consider...	Students learn in different ways...

	Informal	Formal
5	It's high time we all did the right thing.	Downloading songs infringes on the interests of their authors.
6	We can't see and touch the goods.	Daily life is influenced by...
7	When we download songs we cheat their authors of income.	The current situation requires action from all citizens...
8	We, Chinese, do things our own way.	Personally, I favour...
9	I love/ I like/ prefer...	It is important to consider...
10	We face a huge danger of being cheated...	Chinese people tend to do things in a certain way.
11	You may ask...	Many things can be done/are possible...
12	Students have their own styles of learning...	There is a serious risk of fraud...
13	We can do many things...	One may ask...

Exercise 4

Match the formal phrases in the boxes on the right with the informal phrases on the left.

	Informal	Formal
1	Life is not a rose garden. Life is tough.	The trend of globalisation makes it necessary for many people to...
2	On top of that...	To state it briefly / In brief,...
3	In a nutshell...	The points for and against...
4	Last but not least...	Incidentally...
5	Government must make laws...	Life presents a number of challenges.
6	Hong Kong is an international city, so we all must...	There are advantages and disadvantages to...
7	Every coin has two sides.	Another point is that...
8	By the way...	There is a need for laws...
9	Pros & cons of...	Cooperation between the Government and the public is vital...
10	Government & the people must join hands together...	A final and equally/very important point is...

Exercise 5

Replace the phrasal verbs in the sentences with a more appropriate verb from the list below. Don't forget to keep the same tense.

fluctuate   investigate   eliminate   raise   reduce   propose   intervene   establish

1. Researchers have been **looking into** the problem for 15 years. _____
2. This issue was **brought up** during the seminar. _____
3. It is assumed that the management knows what is happening and will therefore **step in** if

there is a problem. _____
4. Schools cannot altogether **get rid of** the problem of truancy. _____
5. The number of staff has been **cut down** recently. _____
6. It was very difficult to **find out** exactly what happened. _____
7. House prices have a tendency to **go up and down**. _____
8. A potential solution was **put forward** two years ago. _____

Exercise 6

Replace the following phrasal verbs with a more formal single word.
1. The locals could not **put up with** the visitors from the city. _____
2. The decline was **brought about** by cheap imports. _____
3. The university is **thinking about** installing CCTV. _____
4. Sales are likely to **drop off** in the third quarter. _____
5. He **went on** speaking for over an hour. _____
6. The meeting was **put off** until December. _____
7. The cinema was **pulled down** ten years ago. _____
8. People have **cut down on** their consumption of beef. _____

Exercise 7

Which of the two alternatives in bold do you think is more appropriate in academic writing ?

1. The government has made **considerable/great** progress in solving the problem.
2. We **got/obtained** excellent results in the experiment.
3. The results of **lots of/numerous** tests have been pretty good/encouraging.
4. A loss of jobs is one of the **consequences/things** that will happen if the process is automated.
5. The relationship between the management and workers is **extremely/really** important.
6. Some suggestions **springing up from/arising from** the study will be presented.

Exercise 8

Use a more formal word or phrase to replace those in bold.
1. The reaction of the officials was **sort of** negative. _____
2. The economic outlook is **nice**. _____
3. Car manufacturers are planning a **get together** to discuss their strategy. _____
4. The resulting competition between countries is **good**. _____
5. The economy is affected by **things** that happen outside the country. _____
6. She was **given the sack** because of her poor record. _____
7. The examination results were **super**. _____

Exercise 9

Replace the contractions in the following sentences with full forms where necessary.

1. The results weren't very encouraging. _____
2. We'll have to conduct another experiment. _____
3. She's been all around the world. _____
4. It's the best solution to the problem. _____
5. Our questionnaire shows that teachers aren't paid what they're worth. _____
6. His response was, "A job's a job; if it doesn't pay enough, it's a lousy job'." _____
7. He'd rather announce the findings at the conference. _____
8. The department's approach didn't succeed. _____

Exercise 10

Suggest improvements to the following sentences to avoid use of "you" and "we".
1. You can apply the same theory of learning to small children. _____
2. You can only do this after the initial preparation has been conducted. _____
3. The figures are accurate to within 1%, but you should note that local variations may apply. _____
4. In the second section of the report, we will consider the environmental consequences. _____

Exercise 11

Suggest alternatives to the following to avoid use of personal language.
1. In this essay I will discuss the main differences between the English and Scottish legal systems.
2. I have divided my report into five sections.
3. I will conclude by proposing that all drugs should be legalized.
4. The opinion of the present author in this essay is that the importance of the monarchy should be reduced.
5. In the third part of the essay, we will look at the reasons for public hysteria over the SARS virus.
6. Although I am not an expert in the field, I have tried very hard to understand the main ideas.

Exercise 12

Make these statements more cautious.
1. Today everyone uses credit cards for all their shopping. _____
2. Drinking wine is bad for you. _____
3. Global warming will have disastrous consequences for the whole world. _____
4. Teleworking leads to isolation. _____
5. Women are worse drivers than men. _____

Exercise 13

Rewrite the following in a more formal style.

1. The positive feedback made up for the problems we came across during the trials.
   _____

2. You can clearly see the differences between these two learning processes.
   _____

3. The subjects didn't have much difficulty with the task. _____

4. We found example after example of autonomous systems in lots of countries.
   _____

Unit 5　Steps in writing a research paper

5.1　Introduction

To write a good research paper, you must be specific about your topic, know what you want to say, and say it effectively. Researchers often follow the following steps to write a good research paper.

(1) Select a topic;
(2) Narrowing down the topic;
(3) Find source;
(4) Evaluate sources;
(5) Take notes;
(6) Ask a research question;
(7) Formulating a thesis statement;
(8) Developing an outline;
(9) Writing the first draft;
(10) Revising the paper.

5.2　Selecting a research topic

The ability to develop a good research topic is an important skill. Sometimes instructors will assign a specific topic, usually you have to select a topic that interests you.

The first thing to do when looking for a research topic is to find a subject area that interests you. Selecting a good topic is not easy. It must be narrow and focused enough to be interesting, yet broad enough to find adequate information for your research.

5.3　Narrowing down the topic

There are two frequently used ways to narrow down a topic. One is to ask questions about the key elements in the topic, the other is to limit it by categories. The goal of the process is to **focus on one specific area of the topic** to study.

If your topic seems too broad, consider questions like:
Is there a specific time period you want to cover?
Is there a geographic region or country on which you would like to focus?
Is there a particular aspect of this topic that interests you?
Example:
Original Topic: Government funding of the arts (**too broad**)
Focused Time Period: 1930s
Focused Location: USA
Focused Event/Aspect: New Deal, painting

Refined topic: Federal funding of painters through New Deal programs and the Works Progress Administration.

The second way to narrow down a topic and make it manageable is to limit your topic.

If you are to write about the topic "environment", common ways to limit the topic are:

By geographic region

Example: What environmental issues are most important in the Southwestern United States?

By culture

Example: How does the environment fit into the Navajo world view?

By time frame

Example: What are the most prominent environmental issues of the last 10 years?

By discipline

Example: How does environmental awareness effect business practices today?

By population group

Example: What are the effects of air pollution on senior citizens?

5.4 Developing a research question

It is absolutely essential to develop a research question that you're interested in or care about in order to focus your research and your paper. How do you develop a usable research question? Choose an appropriate topic or issue for your research, one that actually can be researched. Then list all of the questions that you'd like answered yourself. Choose the best question, one that is neither too broad nor too narrow.

If you know a lot about the topic, you can develop a research question based on your own knowledge. Once you determine what you do know, then you're ready to do some general reading in a textbook or encyclopedia in order to develop a usable research question.

5.5 Finding sources

Once you have defined your research question, it is time to begin researching the topic. There are a variety of sources that you can use to create your research paper. Your primary places for locating sources will be:

The library

Computer sources (CD-ROMs, etc.)

The Internet/World Wide Web

Using sources to support your ideas is one characteristic of the research paper that sets it apart from personal and creative writing. Sources come in many forms, such as magazine and journal articles, books, newspapers, videos, films, computer discussion groups, surveys, or interviews. The important thing is to find and then match appropriate, valid sources to your own ideas.

5.6 Evaluating sources

It's not enough just to find sources; you need to ask both specific as well as general questions to determine whether your source answers your research question. There are four questions to ask when evaluating sources.

1. How well does the source answer the research question?

The way you decide if the source has appropriate information for you is by consulting the table of contents and indexes in a book; in an article read the captions under pictures and diagrams, and then read the first sentence of every paragraph.

2. Is the information provided by an expert?

You want to consider your sources' credentials. A person who has considerable experience and training in an area is an expert. That expert's informed opinion can greatly substantiate your point of view.

3. Is the source valid? Is the information presented objectively from an unbiased viewpoint?

You need to ask these questions to make sure that your sources are good ones to use.

4. Are there a variety of sources?

Another thing to keep in mind is that you want to collect a variety of perspectives and opinions on your topic. Therefore you won't want to rely too heavily on one author, or look for material on just one aspect of your topic.

5.7 Taking notes

Because you will put some of the ideas you get from your research into your research paper, you have to take notes in your reading of the different sources. First of all, make sure that you record all necessary and appropriate information: author(s), title, publisher, place of publication, volume, span of pages, date. Also keep a list of page numbers as you take notes, so you can identify the exact location of each piece of noted information.

Note-taking is the process of extracting only the information that answers your research question or supports your working thesis directly. Notes can be in one of three forms: summary, paraphrase, or direct quotations. Also, a direct quotation reproduces the source's words and punctuation exactly, so you add quotation marks around the sentence(s) to show this. Remember it is essential to record the exact page numbers of the specific notes, since you will need them later for your documentation.

After you take notes, re-read them. Then re-organize them by putting similar information together. Working with your notes involves re-grouping them by topic instead of by source. Grouping your notes should enable you to outline the major sections and then the paragraph of your research paper.

5.8 Developing a research thesis

The research paper begins with a thesis. The thesis statement or hypothesis is the "answer" to your research question. Just as it is important to take the time to create an interesting and researchable "question" your thesis or hypothesis should reflect a similar amount of effort.

The thesis has distinctive characteristics. When you are writing a research paper, there should be one complete sentence that expresses the main idea of your paper. That sentence is often called the thesis statement. Based on everything you've read, and thought, and brainstormed, the thesis is not just your topic, but what you're saying about your topic. Another way to look at it is, once you've come up with the central question, or organizing question, of your paper, the thesis is an answer to that question.

The thesis prepares the reader for the rest of the paper. The thesis statement usually comes within the introductory paragraph, which prepares the reader to listen to your ideas, and before the body of the paper, which develops the thesis with reasons, explanations, and evidence or examples. In fact, if you examine a well-written thesis, you will find hidden in it the questions your reader will expect you to answer in the body.

5.9 Creating an outline

An outline is an organizational tool used by writers to gather thoughts so that they can be clearly laid out in an essay or book. By creating an outline for a piece of writing, the author ensures that all the ideas are presented in a logical, clear order, and that they flow well, drawing the reader to a logical conclusion. An outline can also be used to identify and eliminate potential areas of weakness or lack of focus in a paper.

To sum up, an outline
- Aids in the process of writing
- Helps you organize your ideas
- Presents your material in a logical form
- Shows the relationships among ideas in your writing
- Constructs an ordered overview of your writing
- Defines boundaries and groups

5.10 Writing the first draft

This step of writing is the composition of the text. The most important thing to do is to express thoughts and ideas in a clear and structured way. Make sure that you stay on topic, maintain logical arguments, and include transitions in the writing process.

5.11 Revision

Revision is the final step to take before you finish writing your research paper. The goals for revision are, first, to examine the paper to find out mistakes in the writing;

second, to enable an effective an accurate presentation of ideas; and thirdly, to make the paper as good as it can be by making certain that the arguments are strong and the written expression is accurate.

Exercise 1

What is the last step in writing a research paper? Why is this stage important?

Exercise 2

Narrow down the following research topics.

Exercise is good for you.

Driving a car can be hazardous.

Exercise 3

Narrow down the following topics, following the examples given.

Example:

General topic: Fashion

What **time period** do you want to cover?

Fashion in the 1920s

On what **geographic region** do you want to focus?

Fashion in Japan

On what **person or group of people** do you want to focus?

Fashion for young people

What **particular aspects** of your topic interest you: historical, sociological, psychological, etc.?

Fashion and social status, fashion and women's liberation movement, fashion and self-confidence

Now, please do the same for the following topics.

1. Music   2. Food   3. Animals   4. Movies

Exercise 4

Choose the best research thesis.

Thesis A:

Shakespeare intended the audience to question the existence of Hamlet's father's ghost.

Thesis B:

The appearance of Hamlet's father's ghost raises an important psychological as well as dramatic dilemma in the play.

Thesis C:

Critics through the ages have debated the significance of Hamlet's father's ghost.

Exercise 5

Distinguish between summaries and paraphrases.

Below is a quotation followed by two samples. Identify what each sample is (a paraphrase or a summary).

Quotation:

"Empire State College has a policy describing the conditions under which students may be warned or withdrawn from the college for such unethical academic behavior as plagiarism, forgery, misrepresentation, or other dishonest or deceptive acts which constitute grounds for warning or administrative withdrawal".

Samples:

1. The Student Handbook states that the college may dismiss students who in any way present others' work as their own.
2. According to policy in the Student Handbook, Empire State College may take punitive action (including dismissal) against students who act fraudulently. Fraudulent action includes using the words or ideas of others without proper attribution, falsifying documents, or depicting the words of others as one's own.

Unit 6 Developing an outline

6.1 Functions of an outline

Outlines help the writer organize his/her material logically by helping him/her sort and classify the material systematically. A secondary outcome of the process of sorting and classification is the ability to see the relationships that exist between ideas in our writing. This insight helps the writer develop a organized plan of presenting the material. Outlines, in all their forms, serve four basic functions:
- to present a logical, general description,
- to summarize schematically,
- to reveal an organizational pattern, and
- to provide a visual and conceptual design of the writing.

An outline reflects logical thinking and correct classification.

6.2 Beginning an outline

Before we begin to write an outline, we must have already had a clear picture of at least three things:
- the **purpose** of our paper,
- the **thesis** of our paper, and
- our **audience**.

Then, we can brainstorm and list all the ideas we want to include in this writing, organize our work by grouping ideas together that are related to each other, order our work by dividing the material into groups ranging from the general to the specific, or from abstract to concrete, and label the work by creating main and subtopic headings and writing coordinate levels in parallel form.

6.3 Four features of an outline

An outline has a balanced structure which uses the principles of parallelism, coordination, subordination, and division.

6.3.1 Parallelism

Whenever possible, in writing an outline, **coordinate heads** should be expressed in parallel form. That is, nouns should be made parallel with nouns, verb forms with verb forms, adjectives with adjectives, and so on. Although parallel structure is desired, logical and clear writing should not be sacrificed simply to maintain parallelism (For example, there are times when nouns and gerunds used at the same level of an outline are acceptable). Reasonableness and flexibility of form is preferred to rigidity.

6.3.2　Coordination

In outlining, those items which are of equal significance have comparable numeral or letter designations; an A is equal a B, a 1 to a 2, an a to a b, etc. Coordinates should be seen as "having the same importance." Coordination is a principle that enables the writer to maintain a coherent and consistent document.

Correct coordination
A. Word processing programs
B. Data base programs
C. Spreadsheet programs

Incorrect coordination
A. Word processing programs
B. *Word*
C. *Excel*

Word is a type of word processing program and should be treated as a subdivision. *Excel* is a type of spreadsheet program. One way to correct coordination would be:

A. Types of programs
　　1. *Word*
　　2. *Excel*
B. Evaluation of programs
　　1. *Word*
　　2. *Excel*

6.3.3　Subordination

In order to indicate relevance, that is levels of significance, an outline uses major and minor heading. Thus in ordering ideas you should organize material from general to specific or from abstract to concrete — the more general or abstract the concept, the higher the level or rank in the outline. This principle allows your material to be ordered in terms of logic and requires a clear articulation of the relationship between component parts used in the outline. Subdivisions of a major division should always have the same relationship to the whole.

Correct subordination
A. Word processing programs
　　1. *Word*
　　2. *WordPerfect*
B. Presentation programs
　　1. *MS Power Point*
　　2. *Corel Presentations*

Faulty subordination
A. Word processing programs

1. *WordPerfect*
2. Useful
3. Obsolete

There is an A without a B. Also 1, 2, 3 are not equal; *WordPerfect* is a type of word processing program, and useful and obsolete are qualities. One way to correct this faulty subordination is:

A. *WordPerfect*
   1. Positive features
   2. Negative features
B. *Word*
   1. Positive features
   2. Negative features

6.3.4 Division

To divide you always need at least two parts; therefore, there can never be an A without a B, a 1 without a 2, an a without a b, etc. Usually there is more than one way to divide parts; however, when dividing use only one basis of division at each rank and make the basis of division as sharp as possible.

Example

A. Microcomputer hardware
   1. Types
   2. Cost
   3. Maintenance
B. Microcomputer software

6.4 Form of the outline

The most important principle for an outline's form is consistency. An outline can use **topic** or **sentence** structure, but be consistent in form all the way through.

A topic outline uses words or phrases for all points; no punctuation is used after entries. It presents a brief overview of work and is generally easier and faster to write than a sentence outline.

A sentence outline uses complete sentences for all entries; correct punctuation should be used after each entry. A sentence outline presents a more detailed overview of work including possible topic sentences; is easier and faster for writing the final paper.

An outline can use either alpha-numeric (usually with Roman numerals) form or a decimal form. Alternating patterns of upper and lower case letters with alternating progressions of Roman and Arabic numerals mark the level of subordination within the alpha-numeric form of the outline. Progressive patterns of decimals mark the levels of subordination in decimal form of outlining. The decimal form has become the standard form in scientific and technical writing. For example,

The alpha-numeric form	The decimal form
I.	1
A.	1.1
B.	1.2
1.	1.2.1
2.	1.2.2
a.	1.2.2.1
b.	1.2.2.2

6.5 Two sample outline that illustrates many of the above-mentioned points

Sample 1

Competitive Swimming, an Ideal Sport for Kids

1. Introduction
2. Competitive swimming provides same benefits as other sports
   a. It is good exercise and builds muscular strength
   b. It promotes cooperation among team members, especially in relays
3. Competitive swimming provides some additional benefits
   a. Swimming is an important skill that can be used forever
   b. There is a reduced risk of injury
   c. Each swimmer can easily chart his or her own progress
4. My personal experience as a competitive swimmer
   a. I enjoy working with my coach
   b. I've made a lot of friends on the swim team
5. Conclusion

Sample 2

The Conquest of Mt. Everest

Ⅰ. Introduction
Ⅱ. Background information
  A. Location of Mt. Everest
  B. Geography of the surrounding area
  C. Facts about Mt. Everest
    1. Height of the mountain
    2. How the mountain was named
      a. Peak XV
      b. Joloungma (Tibetan name)
      c. Sagarmatha (Nepalese name)
    3. The number of people who have climbed Everest to date
Ⅲ. Major explorers covered in this paper
  A. Sir Edmund Hillary

        1. First to reach the summit (1953)
        2. Led a team of experienced mountain climbers who worked together
    B. Tenzing Norgay and the Sherpas
        1. Norgay was an experienced climber and guide who accompanied Hillary
        2. Sherpas still used to guide expeditions
    C. Rob Hall
        1. Leader of the failed 1996 expedition
        2. Led group of (mainly) tourists with little mountain climbing experience
IV. The impact expeditions have had on Mt. Everest and local community
    A. Ecological effects
        1. Loss of trees due to high demand for wood for cooking and heating for tourists.
        2. Piles of trash left by climbing expeditions
    B. Economic effects
        1. Expedition fees provide income for the country
        2. Expeditions provide work for the Sherpas, contributing to the local economy.
    C. Cultural effects
        1. Introduction of motor vehicles
        2. Introduction of electricity
V. Conclusion

Exercise 1

Arrange the information in the following outline in the right format.

The College Application Process

I. Choose Desired Colleges

A. Visit and evaluate college campuses

B. Visit and evaluate college websites

1. look for interesting classes

2. note important statistics

a. student/faculty ratio

b. retention rate

II. Prepare Application

A. Write Personal Statement

1. Choose interesting topic

a. describe an influential person in your life

(1) favorite high school teacher

(2) grandparent

2. Include important personal details

a. volunteer work

b. participation in varsity sports

B. Revise personal statement

Ⅲ. Compile resume
A. List relevant coursework
B. List work experience
C. List volunteer experience
1. tutor at foreign language summer camp
2. counselor for suicide prevention hotline

Exercise 2

Write an outline for a presentation on the benefits of distance learning (online classes) from a student's perspective. The audience will be students and teachers with very little computer experience and may be somewhat fearful of the idea.

Unit 7 Writing academic paragraphs

7.1 Topic sentences and their support in a paragraph

A paragraph is a group of related sentences, which develop one main idea (**the topic sentence**). The topic sentence tends to be a general rather than a specific idea. The main idea of the topic sentence controls the rest of the paragraph. Usually it is the first sentence in the paragraph, but not necessarily. It may come after a transition sentence; it may even come at the end of a paragraph.

Topic sentences are not the only way to organise a paragraph, and not all paragraphs need a topic sentence. For example, paragraphs that describe, narrate, or detail the steps in an experiment do not usually need topic sentences. They are useful, however, in paragraphs that analyse and argue. They are particularly useful for writers who have difficulty developing focused, unified paragraphs (i.e. writers who tend to waffle). Topic sentences help these writers develop a main idea for their paragraphs and most importantly stay focused. Topic sentences also help guide the reader through complex arguments.

The **supporting sentences** in a paragraph develop the main idea expressed in the topic sentence and provide the detail such as facts and examples. When the topic sentence comes first, the supporting sentences answer the questions the reader will develop in their minds after reading the topic sentence. In this case, the last sentence (**concluding sentence**) can either return the reader to the topic at the beginning of the paragraph or act as a connection to link the information with that coming up in the next paragraph. When the topic sentence comes last, the supporting sentences build up arguments and examples to make a case for the main idea contained at the end.

7.2 Building a paragraph

7.2.1 Logical order

A well constructed paragraph contains sentences that are logically arranged and flow smoothly. Logical arrangement refers to the order of your sentences and ideas. There are various ways to order your sentences, depending on your purpose. For example, if you want to describe historical background to an event or something that happened to you, you would order your sentences according to the sequence of action, from beginning to end. However, if you want to describe important points to your argument you may want to start with the most important point first and arrange the following point according to level of importance.

7.2.2 Linking

Not only should sentences and ideas in a paragraph be logically arranged, but they should also flow smoothly. Expressions such as *next*, *then*, *after*, *when* and other signal time sequence; expressions such as *an example of*, *the most significant example*, *to illustrate* are used to identify the example in the sentence. Such expressions provide a link between the ideas presented. Although you do not need to include a linking word or phrase in every sentence, you should use enough of them to help your reader follow your ideas clearly.

7.2.3 Repetition of key words

Each sentence in a paragraph should relate to the topic and develop the main idea. If a sentence does not relate to or develop that idea. If your paragraph repeats and elaborates key words there is less chance of writing irrelevant material. Consider the topic sentence: ***Smoking cigarettes can be an expensive habit***. The following sentences in the paragraph need to discuss why smoking is expensive, both from a financial as well as a health point of view. Repeating the key words "*smoking*" and "*expensive*" or finding synonyms for these words allows you to keep your writing focussed on the main idea of a paragraph.

7.2.4 Relevance

If a sentence does not relate to or develop the main idea, it is irrelevant and should be omitted. Cutting out the irrelevant material is part of the task of revising. Consider the topic sentence: ***Smoking cigarettes can be an expensive habit***. If a sentence in the paragraph discusses how to blow smoke rings, it is out of place; it does not discuss the expense of smoking. A paragraph that has sentences that do not relate to or discuss the main idea lack unity.

7.3 Incorporating sources within paragraphs

The point of view a writer develops in an essay and within each paragraph cannot just be based on personal opinion, but must be backed up with evidence, examples and the opinion of experts. The words or ideas taken from other sources need to be clearly signaled as belonging to another person. This is done by referring to the author as well as the source of the words or ideas.

At the whole essay level the point of view is called the **thesis statement**. Within a paragraph the point of view is often broadly expressed in the **topic sentence**. The topic sentence is often **re-stated** within the paragraph with more specific detail given and **evidence** provided in support of the point of view, usually from the reading done for the essay. The **sources referred to** back up the writer. Any **additional comments** by the writer should aim to make the writer's point of view clear.

7.4 Different types of paragraphs in a research paper

There are three main types of paragraphs in an academic research paper: **introductory paragraphs**, the **body paragraphs** and the **concluding paragraphs**. These types of paragraphs are located in the introduction, the body of the paper or in the conclusion, respectively. Each of these types of paragraphs fulfils a different function for the reader.

The **introductory paragraph(s)** provides the reader with any necessary background information before leading into a clear statement of the writer's point of view. The point of view, or thesis statement, is a brief but very specific statement of the position the writer will take in the paper. The introductory paragraph may also present an overall plan of the way the research paper's argument will be developed, as well as any limits the writer will place on the topic.

The **body paragraphs** which follow all flow logically from the introductory paragraph. They expand on the thesis statement and each in turn is clearly focused on a single issue with plenty of supporting detail or evidence from concrete and relevant examples, or from the reading which the writer uses to support the point of view. Arguments by other writers against the point of view taken by the research paper writer should also be presented (and argued against) in the body paragraphs. The body paragraphs carefully build up the writer's point of view in detail.

The **concluding paragraph(s)** summarises the points made, repeats the overall point of view, and explains why the writer took the position held. It may also indicate wider issues not covered in the research paper but of interest and relevant to the point of view.

7.5 Developing paragraphs

There are several ways in which you can build good, clear paragraphs. This section will discuss three of the most common types of paragraph structure: development by detail, comparison and contrast, and process. Finally, it will suggest that most paragraphs are built of a combination of development strategies.

7.5.1 Paragraph development by detail

This is the most common and easiest form of paragraph development: you simply expand on a general topic sentence using specific examples or illustrations. Look at the following paragraph.

Work tends to be associated with non-work-specific environments, activities, and schedules. If asked what space is reserved for learning, many students would suggest the classroom, the lab or the library. What about the kitchen? The bedroom? In fact, any room in which a student habitually studies becomes a learning space, or a place associated with thinking. Some people need to engage in sports or other physical activity before they can work successfully. Being sedentary seems to inspire others. Although most classes are scheduled between 8:30 and 22:00, some students do their best work before the sun rises, some after it sets. Some need a less flexible schedule than others, while a very few can sit and not rise until their task is completed. Some students work quickly and efficiently, while others cannot produce anything without much dust and heat.

The topic sentence makes a general claim: that school work tends not to be associated only with school. The rest of the sentences provide various illustrations of this argument. They are organised around the three categories, "environment, activities, and schedules", enumerated in the topic sentence. The details provide the concrete examples which your reader will use to evaluate the credibility of your topic sentence.

7.5.2 Paragraph development by comparison and contrast

You should consider developing your paragraph by comparison and contrast when you are describing two or more things which have something, but not everything, in common. You may choose to compare either point by point (X is big, Y is little; X and Y are both purple.) or subject by subject (X is big and purple; Y is small and purple.). Consider, for example, the following paragraph.

Although the interpretation of traffic signals may seem highly standardized, close observation reveals regional variations across this country, distinguishing the East Coast from Central Canada and the West as surely as dominant dialects or political inclinations. In Montreal, a flashing red traffic light instructs drivers to careen even more wildly through intersections heavily populated with pedestrians and oncoming vehicles. In startling contrast, an amber light in Calgary warns drivers to scream to a halt on the off chance that there might be a pedestrian within 500 meters who might consider crossing at some unspecified time within the current day. In my home town in New Brunswick, finally, traffic lights (along with painted lines and posted speed limits) do not apply to tractors, all terrain vehicles, or pickup trucks, which together account for most vehicles on the road. In fact, were any observant Canadian dropped from an alien space vessel at an unspecified intersection anywhere in this vast land, he or she could almost certainly orient him-or-herself according to the surrounding traffic patterns.

This paragraph compares traffic patterns in three areas of Canada. It contrasts the behaviour of drivers in the Maritimes, in Montreal, and in Calgary, in order to make a point about how attitudes in various places inform behaviour. People in these areas have in common the fact that they all drive; in contrast, they drive differently according to the area in which they live.

It is important to note that the paragraph above considers only one aspect of driving (behaviour at traffic lights). If you wanted to consider two or more aspects, you would probably need more than one paragraph.

7.5.3 Paragraph development by process

Paragraph development by process involves a straightforward step-by-step description. Those of you in the sciences will recognise it as the formula followed in the "method" section of a lab experiment. Process description often follows a chronological sequence.

The first point to establish is the grip of the hand on the rod. This should be about half-way up the cork handle, absolutely firm and solid, but not tense or rigid. All four fingers are curved around the handle, the little finger, third finger and middle finger contributing most of the firmness by pressing the cork solidly into the fleshy part of the palm, near the heel of the hand. The forefinger supports and steadies the grip but supplies its own firmness against the thumb, which should be along the upper side of the handle and somewhere near the top of the grip.

The topic sentence establishes that the author will use this paragraph to describe the process of establishing the "grip of the hand on the rod," and this is exactly what he does, point by point, with little abstraction.

7.5.4 Paragraph development by combination

Very often, a single paragraph will contain development by a combination of methods. It may begin with a brief comparison, for example, and move on to provide detailed descriptions of the subjects being compared. A process analysis might include a brief history of the process in question. Many paragraphs include lists of examples.

The broad range of positive characteristics used to define males could be used to define females too, but they are not. At its entry for woman Webster's Third provides a list of "qualities considered distinctive of womanhood": "Gentleness, affection, and domesticity or on the other hand fickleness, superficiality, and folly." Among the "qualities considered distinctive of manhood" listed in the entry for man, no negative attributes detract from the "courage, strength, and vigor" the definers associate with males. According to this dictionary, womanish means "unsuitable to a man or to a strong character of either sex."

This paragraph is a good example of one which combines a comparison and contrast of contemporary notions of "manliness" and "womanliness" with an extended list of examples.

Exercise 1

Identify the **topic sentences** in the following paragraphs.

1. Adventure tourism is a different way for tourists to see New Zealand. This type of tourism uses the plentiful natural resources — mountains, rivers, lakes, wilderness areas and historical sites to provide adventure, thrills and challenges which are low risk but high in excitement. For example, the coastal areas in New Zealand are great for canoeing and kayaking. White-water rafting is another popular water adventure tour. However, if you would rather keep your feet on the ground, New Zealand has over 100 developed walkways in addition to the tracks in the 12 National Parks. Because more and more tourists are interested in learning about New Zealand by doing exciting and unusual activities, adventure tourism will continue to grow.

2. No matter how you slice it, there are only 24 hours in a day. To be successful at university, students need to learn good time-management skills. The first skill is not taking on more than you can handle. If you are a working part-time, have a family and are involved in a community organisation, then taking a full course-load at university

will be too much. Another time management skill is reasonably estimating the time required to perform each of the tasks at hand. For example, deeply reading a chapter from a course text cannot be completed in between television programmes. Finally, actually *doing* what needs to be done seems obvious, but is a very difficult skill. You may find that cleaning out your wardrobe becomes vital when you are avoiding study. Procrastination is a time manager's enemy. By learning time management skills your university study will be successful and most importantly enjoyable.

3. The heart weighs about 11 ounces and is the size of a clenched fist. The heart of a man performs at about 60 to 80 beats a minute. In a year it beats some 40 million times. At each beat it takes in nearly a quarter of a pint of blood; in a single day it pumps 2 200 gallons of blood, and in the course of a single lifetime about 56 million gallons. Is there any other engine capable of carrying on such heavy work over such a long period of time without needing to be repaired? Obviously the human heart is a small yet highly efficient piece of equipment.

Exercise 2

Read the following paragraphs carefully. Then write an appropriate **topic sentence** for each of the paragraphs.

1. Thousands of new people are born on our planet every day. The number of inhabitants in the world has already reached over six billion. If the present growth rate remains unchecked, the world may soon face wide-spread starvation, poverty, and serious health problems. _____. (topic sentence)

2. _____. (topic sentence)
Arriving in the land below the Rio Grande River, the Spanish conquistador Hernando Cortez was surprised to see the local inhabitants raising crops that included avocados, corn, garlic and nuts. Onions, tomatoes, chilli peppers and pumpkins were also grown in the rich soil. Irrigation systems were employed in some of the drier regions. The Aztec farmers also were skilful in creating terraced gardens to make the most of the rainfall and to minimise soil erosion. Evidence shows that they employed crop rotation as well as natural fertilisers to enhance the production of their farm products.

Exercise 3

The **topic sentence** of each of the following paragraphs has been omitted. After a careful reading, write your own topic sentence for each.

1. The most important factor is a student's past experience of study. If a student has already developed good study habits, study at university should not be difficult. Good study habits need to be complemented by interest and motivation, factors which are important when competition gets tough. We should however not underestimate the distracting effects of financial and personal difficulties. All students have to grapple with these at some stage of their university life. Beyond the personal factors it has to be

said that there is also a certain element of luck involved in success: this includes finding excellent teachers and the subject matter that inspires one to give one's best.

_____

2. Animal breeding for particular features may soon become obsolete with the new-found ability of scientists to work at the level of genes. On the one hand there are those who embrace the new bio-technology: genetic engineering. They argue that many genetic changes will be hugely beneficial and harmless. As long as safeguards are in place, they claim, humans would be foolish not to take advantage of the many benefits genetic engineering has to offer. Others have seen the speed with which gene manipulation can get out of hand, mixing species so that vegetable and animal are no longer distinguishable. They want to wind the clock back. But can they?

_____

Exercise 4

Put the following sentences into logical order to build a coherent paragraph.

1. a. In these rural areas 70 percent of the available agricultural land suffers from dryness and lack of irrigation.
   b. As a result, the crops are usually marginal with hardly enough production to feed the farmer's family.
   c. The first fact to consider is that over 60 percent of the population live in rural communities.
   d. In my country, one of the most urgent problems facing the government today relates to agriculture.
   e. And without irrigation, agricultural production is wholly dependent on the uncertain rainfall.
   f. To understand the nature of this problem one has to look at some of the facts.

   _____

2.
   a. It may be the succession of summers with extremely high temperatures that is to blame.
   b. Added to this is the costly array of cooling power drinks that New Yorkers now consume to keep body temperatures down.
   c. The result is high and unwelcome summer electricity and food bills.
   d. New Yorkers have recently been complaining that the cost of keeping cool in summer has sky rocketed.
   e. The cost of running an air-conditioner non-stop in the unrelenting heat has doubled over the last five years.
   f. Electricity prices are the main reason for the chorus of complaints.
   g. The refrigerator too is having to work overtime.

   _____

Exercise 5

In the following paragraph, the linking words and phrases are left out. Add the words and phrases that you think make sense.

Living in one's ethnic community in a new land is very pleasant, ___(1)___ it definitely has some disadvantages. Let me explain what I mean through personal example. At first, when I came from China to Auckland, I was very happy because some of my old friends were living in the same neighborhood. A year later, ___(2)___, my family and I decided to move from that area in order to live near where we worked. That day I began to feel that I was living in another country, in another Auckland. My first problem came when I tried to tell my landlord that our refrigerator was broken. He didn't speak Mandarin, — ___(3)___ I didn't speak English. Little things like that made me feel unhappy and insecure, ___(4)___ I did not want to go back to my own ethnic community. I was living in a new country, ___(5)___ I had to do things for myself. I had to learn a different culture, a different language, and different customs. Living with my ethnic group was very comfortable, ___(6)___ at the same time it was harmful ___(7)___ I didn't learn some of the essentials for survival in a new country. It was an important, though painful, lesson to learn.

Exercise 6

In the following paragraphs coherence is achieved by repetition of key words. Find the key words in the paragraph.

When surnames began appearing in Europe 800 years ago, a person's identity and occupation were often intertwined. A surname was a direct link between who the person was and what he/she did. Taylor is the Old English spelling of tailor, and Clark is derived from clerk, an occupation of considerable status during the Middle Ages because it required literacy. The names Walker, Wright, Carter, Stewart and Turner indicate occupations. A walker was someone who cleaned cloth; a wright was a carpenter or metalworker; a carter was someone who drove a cart; a steward was a person in charge of a farm or estate; and a turner worked a lathe. One of the few occupational surnames reflecting the work of women is Webster, which refers to a female weaver.

Exercise 7

In the following paragraph the topic sentence is highlighted in bold. Underline the sentence or sentences that do not belong to the paragraph. There may be one or more irrelevant sentences.

Another problem facing a number of elderly people is living on a reduced income. When they retire, old people may receive a pension from their company or a benefit from the government. The amount of their monthly income is often significantly less than they received when they were fully employed. All of a sudden, retirees find that they can no longer continue the life style that they had become accustomed to, even if that life style was a modest one. Many find, after paying their monthly bills, that there is no money left for a movie or dinner out. Of course, sometimes they can not go out because of their health. They may have arthritis or rheumatism and it is painful for them to move around. This can also limit their lifestyle. For some elderly people, however, the small amount of money they receive will not even cover their monthly bills. They realise with horror that electricity, a telephone, and good food are luxuries they can no longer afford. They resort to living in cold homes, and eating cheap food to make ends meet.

Exercise 8

Find out the following elements in the following paragraphs:

Topic sentence

Evidence in support of topic sentence

Source of evidence

Writer's comments

1.

Year by year more students are borrowing money for their education, and they are borrowing more money. In the first year of the loan scheme 45 000 students had loans. By 1999 the number had grown to 300 000. Two years ago, the average loan debt was NZ $ 5 000. It is now $ 10 600, according to figures supplied by the Alliance Party (Gordon, 1999). The total levels of student debt have reached unsustainable levels for the New Zealand economy.

2.

Topic sentence

Restatement of topic with more specific detail

Evidence in support of topic sentence

Source of evidence

Writer's comments

It now appears that many students are leaving New Zealand to escape their student loan repayments. This is particularly acute as a problem in the information technology field. A computer company director has recently reported that graduates who work in his company leave New Zealand after working for only one or two years and that "when we do the exit interview, we find that they're leaving not just because they believe they can get more money, but to escape paying back the student loans." (Gifford, 1999, July 28, p. C1). Surely the government will have to address this problem urgently, especially if the problem is widespread.

Exercise 9

In the following paragraph the supporting evidence is missing. Choose one of the following quotations from David Crystal's *English as a Global Language* for inserting into this

paragraph at the place indicated with "...". Its purpose is to lend support to the argument being made by the writer.

When Britain was a colonial power its military might ensured that the English language remained as a lasting influence on the many cultures it came into contact with. Britain is no longer a powerful force yet English remains the dominant world language. The explanation is simple. As David Crystal states, "...". English is now maintained as the dominant world language by the economic powerhouse of the world's richest nation, the USA.

"By the beginning of the nineteenth, Britain had become the world's leading industrial and trading country" (Crystal, 1997, p.8).

"British political imperialism had sent English around the globe, during the nineteenth century, so that it was a language 'on which the sun never sets'" (Crystal, 1997, p.8).

"It may take a militarily powerful nation to establish a language, but it takes an economically powerful one to maintain and expand it" (Crystal, 1997, p.7).

Exercise 10

The sentences below come from different kinds of paragraphs in an essay on censorship. Identify each sentence as belonging to an *introductory*, *body or concluding paragraph*.

1. The attitudes which have been discussed in this paper stem from a variety of misconceptions about the notion of personal freedom.
2. The main reason for people being unhappy with censorship in any form comes from their mistaken belief that an individual's private actions have no effect on others.
3. Western countries people have started to become very critical of attempts to restrict personal freedom via censorship.
4. A related reason for dissatisfaction with censorship appears to be a false notion of the idea of freedom of expression of ideas.

Exercise 11

Write down the function of each paragraph in the following essay.
Paragraph 1 _____
Paragraph 2 _____
Paragraph 3 _____
Paragraph 4 _____
Paragraph 5 _____
Paragraph 6 _____

The Cost of Tourism in the Cook Islands

In theory, tourism brings substantial economic benefits to a country. But who gains the wealth generated? In recent times tour operators have brought large numbers of tourists to the Cook Islands to enjoy their beauty and the traditional life style. Local people meet this demand in the form of profit generation. Can it be argued that tourism in the Cook

Islands has brought wealth and well-being for the majority of the local population? Tourism is also promoted as creating jobs and fostering social relations, and in particular a better understanding between nations. However, there is, according to one researcher, "a growing body of empirical evidence that the so-called 'benefits' of tourism are often greatly outweighed by the substantial long-term social and environmental costs incurred" (Mercer, 1994, p. 127). This essay will argue that in the case of the Cook Islands, tourism's economic and social benefits are unfortunately unrealised ideals and that instead it has put stresses and strains on both the country's economic wellbeing and its social values.

Turning first to the alleged economic benefits of tourism, we can see that in the case of the Cook Islands, there is a variety of sources of income from tourist receipts. According to a 1991 visitor survey (Tourism Council of the South Pacific, 1991), after beach activities and natural scenery (62%), visitors to the Cook Islands are looking for entertainment and folklore and culture experiences (27%). Tourists contribute to the local economy by spending money on travel to and around the country, as well as on accommodation, food, entertainment and souvenirs. Results from this same survey, for example, revealed that in the survey period (October 1991 to February 1992) close to 90% of tourists surveyed stayed in hotels or similar accommodation. Also, close to 70% of total tourist expenditure was on accommodation, restaurants and bars, with a further 16% on transport, tours and entertainment (Tourism Council of the South Pacific, 1991). Tourists are thus helping to create jobs which are based on making them feel welcome and at the same time they put cash into the economy directly by paying for services.

There are down sides however. The Cook Islands does not have the capacity to own and maintain businesses such as large airline companies or tourist hotels. They are owned by other countries such as New Zealand or multinational conglomerates. The cost of travel and accommodation, which constitutes a large part of a tourist's expenditure, goes directly to the foreign-owned airlines and hotels. These outside interests draw the bulk of the profit they create out of the country. Little of it reaches the local economy. According to Milne (1987), overseas operators receive approximately 60% of all tourist receipts, while local Europeans receive 23%, with the remaining 17% flowing to Cook Islands owned enterprises. It is likely that these disproportionate shares of control of the tourist dollar will have spin off effects on the social fabric. As Milne claims "the crucial factor in determining the level of negative social impacts is the degree to which local participation in the ownership and control of the industry is undermined" (Milne, 1987, p. 120). Tourism in the Cook Islands in the late eighties appears to have provided overwhelming economic benefit to foreigners rather than the local population. This may well have impacted negatively on the social fabric. It is beyond the scope of the essay to examine this, but Milne's claim seems a reasonable one.

The creation of jobs is often claimed to be one of the positive side effects of tourism. However, according Milne (1987, p. 134) "Despite totalling 95% of the population, Cook

Island Maoris only fill 53% of the managerial or supervisory positions in the industry. Europeans on the other hand, fill 47% of these positions, despite comprising less than 5% of the country's population". Again, there is clearly an imbalance between local and non-local participation in the economic benefits of tourism in terms of who does what job. This mirrors the imbalance in ownership of operator resources described in the previous paragraph. Another unintended negative effect is that tourism employment is seen as easy money when compared to traditional island occupations like cropping. It attracts labour away from cropping, another important source of income for the economy. So Cook Islanders appear mainly to receive economic benefit via mostly non-managerial wages and at the same time the labour force is drawn away from other important areas of economic activity.

Turning to the supposed social benefits of tourism, we can also see some discrepancies beneath the surface ideals. To take advantage of any other money the tourists are prepared to spend, Cook Islanders court tourists with their own enterprises. But tourists have their own set of images about the culture before they even set foot in the country, and when they arrive they seek to affirm these images. Tourists usually only want to see what is pleasant and enjoyable whether or not they are experiencing truly authentic features of a society. This explains for example the popularity of the 'traditional' Cook Island tapa cloths and lava lavas which are imported from a factory in New Zealand. The cost in cultural terms is borne out further by another reality lying behind the ideal. Tourism is claimed to draw different cultures together. However, what often results from this cultural mixing of first and third world populations is cultural envy (Milne, 1987, p. 127). With increased exposure to western lifestyles local people start to emulate aspects of western culture such as consumerism and the consumption of alcohol, with the expected negative results. All of these less than ideal realities beneath a positive surface indicate that as far as the Cook Islands are concerned, for the relatively low financial return that tourism offers to the local population, the social costs are too high.

It is worth considering what economic benefits might be found in less socially damaging and economically more effective forms of the industry. Tuara (1990) for example contains a detailed discussion of an appropriate model for sustainable tourism development based on the experience of Barbados, and in a recent discussion of the role of ecotourism in the Pacific, Hall concludes: "to neglect the social dimension of development and people's relationship to their environment is in opposition to the principles of sustainable development" (1994, p. 154). He cites a study of ecotourism in the Solomon Islands (Rudkin, 1994), where "development proposals served only to reinforce the power and wealth of 'big men' at the expense of the wider indigenous community". The Cook Islands could perhaps avoid the reinforcement of similar existing power relations if tourist planning was more under the control of those affected by it. Control of the Cook Islands tourism industry by local people, training of local people and advice from those outsiders working alongside in a partnership mode could mean that tourism brings many more benefits and fewer costs.

Unit 8　What is an abstract ?

8.1　Definition of an abstract

An abstract is a brief summary of the most important points in a research paper. It is a concise **summary of a larger project** (a thesis, research report, etc.) that concisely describes the content and scope of the project and identifies the project's objective, its methodology and its findings, conclusions, or intended results.

8.2　Functions of an abstract

Abstracts summarized the research study; they assist the reader in deciding whether or not the study meets his or her need; they provide the reader with an overview of the remaining sections of the paper. They enable professionals to stay current with the huge volume of scientific literature.

8.3　Some misconceptions of an abstract

Although the abstract appears first in a paper, it is generally the last part written. Only after the paper has been completed can the authors decide what should be in the abstract and what parts are supporting detail.

Some students have misconceptions about the nature of abstracts. Perhaps the two most common misconceptions are that the abstract is a table of contents or an introduction. An abstract is neither of these. Just because it appears first in a paper does not mean that it is an integral part of the paper. Abstracts should be able to stand alone.

At first glance, it might seem that the introduction and the abstract are very similar because they both present the research problem and objectives as well as briefly reviewing methodology, main findings and main conclusions. However, there are important differences between the two.

Introduction

Should be short, but does not have a word limit;

Main purpose is to introduce the research by presenting its context or background. Introductions usually go from general to specific, introducing the research problem and how it will be investigated).

Abstract

Has a maximum word limit;

Is a summary of the whole research;

Main purpose is to summarize the research (particularly the objective and the main finding/conclusion), NOT to introduce the research area.

Remember that your abstract is a **description of your project** (what you specifically are doing) and not a description of your topic (whatever you're doing the project *on*). It is easy to get these two types of description confused.

As you are writing your abstract, stop at the end of every sentence and make sure you are summarizing **the project you have undertaken** rather than the more general topic.

8.4 Abstracts and others types of summaries

There are a lot of different ways to summarize a scientific article or other document. The title itself is sort of a one-line summary. An outline is also a summary. An "executive summary" is often a statement of the basic idea in simple terms.

An abstract has certain features that set it aside from the above.
- It is always short.
- It is always written as a single paragraph
- It is written for the same audience as the article, so it uses the same level of technical language.
- It always summarizes the major points of the results.
- It ordinarily summarizes the major points of the materials and methods, and of the discussion.

8.5 Differences across disciplines

Abstracts vary from discipline to discipline. However, even within single disciplines, abstracts often differ.

Abstracts in the hard sciences and social sciences often put more emphasis on methods than do abstracts in the humanities; humanities abstracts often spend much more time explaining their objective than science abstracts do.

8.6 Major elements in an abstract

Despite the fact that abstracts vary somewhat from discipline to discipline, every abstract should include four main types of information.
- It should state the main **objective** and rationale of your project,
- it should outline the **methods** you used to accomplish your objectives,
- it should list your project's **results or product**,
- and it should draw **conclusions** about the implications of your project.

However, it's important to note that the weight accorded to the different components can vary by discipline. For models, try to find abstracts of research that is similar to your research.

8.6.1 What should the objective/rationale section look like?

The first few sentences of your abstract should state the **problem you set out to solve** or **the issue you set out to explore** and explain your **rationale or motivation** for pursuing the project. The problem or issue might be a research question, a gap in critical attention to a text, a societal concern, etc. The purpose of your study is to solve this problem and/or add to your discipline's understanding of the issue.

8.6.2 What should the methods section look like?

This section of the abstract should explain how you went about solving the problem or exploring the issue you identified as your main objective.

For a hard science or social science research project, this section should include a concise description of the process by which you conducted your research. For a humanities project, it should make note of any theoretical framework or methodological assumptions.

8.6.3 What should the results/intended results section look like?

This section of the abstract should list the **results** or **outcomes** of the work you have done so far. If your project is not yet complete, you may still want to include preliminary results or your hypotheses about what those results will be.

8.6.4 What should the conclusion section look like?

The abstract should close with a statement of the project's **implications** and **contributions to its field**. It should convince readers that the project is interesting, valuable, and worth investigating further.

8.7 When to write the abstract

The abstract, although it is put first in your research paper, always should be written last. It needs to be written last because it is the essence of your report, drawing information from all of the other sections of the report. It explains why the experiment was performed and what conclusions were drawn from the results obtained.

The best way to attempt to go about writing an abstract is to divide it into the sections mentioned above. The first two sections are very similar and can be grouped together, but do not have to be. If you decide to address them separately, make sure that you do not repeat anything. Often a section can be mentioned in only one sentence. Remember, brevity is the key to a successful abstract. Each section is addressed below to help clarify what needs to be included and what can be omitted.

8.8 How to write an abstract

The most important thing to remember when writing the abstract is to be brief and state only what is pertinent. No extraneous information should be included. A successful abstract is compact, accurate and self-contained. It also must be clear enough so someone who is unfamiliar with your experiment could understand why you did what you did, and what the experiment indicated in the end. An additional note is that abstracts typically are written in the passive voice, but it is acceptable to use personal pronouns such as I or we.

In the objective section of the abstract, you are supposed to tell the reader why the research is done and what problem is being addressed. This section is the statement of the original problem. It is the reason behind why an experiment is being done. This should not include many details, rather it should be a simple statement. It can even be stated in one or two sentences at the most.

In the method section of the abstract you should tell the reader what was done to try to answer the question proposed. It should in no way be very detailed. It contains a brief outline of what was done, highlighting only crucial steps. It is a description of *how* you decided to approach the problem.

The result section should contain only the crucial results obtained. The crucial results are those that are necessary to answer your original question posed. Without these results, the experiment would have been useless. The results should be stated briefly and should not be explained; they should only be mentioned.

The conclusion section is the end of your abstract, directly hinging on the results obtained. This is the "so what" part of your experiment. "So what" refers to what the results mean in the long run. This should directly follow the results so the reader knows what results led to what conclusions. Sometimes you can also mention the implication of the conclusion.

Exercise 1

Identify the objective, method, result and conclusion part in the following abstracts.

1. The basis of this project was to create a garment using mixed media in order to mimic the human body. The materials we used to create this piece include: buckram, copper wire, spray paint, fabric paint, a variety of novelty fabrics, and chains. The techniques we created in order to manipulate the piece include: fabric branding and burning, grid painting, sewing, draping, molding buckram, and coiling. Our overall approach was to create a theatrical wearable art piece. Upon completion of the assignment we found the piece aesthetically pleasing because of the way it molds to the human body, but can be a piece all on its own.

2. The purpose of this study is to identify relationships between the physical and genetic characteristics of bones in mice. The physical characteristics include size, density, and the force required to break the bone, while the genetic ones are the genes of the marker loci associated with the genes that affect these qualities. This study uses strains of mice with reduced genetic variation. The two strains of mice that are the most phenotypically extreme, meaning those with the strongest and weakest bones, are crossed. The F2 generation from that cross is then analyzed. The results of this analysis can be used to find which genotypes correlate with specific bone properties like size, density, and failure load. The anticipated outcome of this lab is the identification of the genotypes that affect bone strength in mice. The findings may be useful in treating medical conditions that are related to bone strength.

3. This project involves discovering how the American Revolution was remembered during

the nineteenth century. The goal is to show that the American Revolution was memorialized by the actions of the United States government during the 1800s. This has been done by examining events such as the Supreme Court cases of John Marshall and the Nullification Crisis. Upon examination of these events, it becomes clear that John Marshall and John Calhoun (creator of the Doctrine of Nullification) attempted to use the American Revolution to bolster their claims by citing speeches from Founding Fathers. Through showing that the American Revolution lives on in memory, this research highlights the importance of the revolution in shaping the actions of the United States government.

4. The study is to show how even a "sport" video game can incorporate many types of learning, to call attention to what might be overlooked as significant forms of learning, and to understand and take advantage of the opportunities video games afford as more deliberate learning environments. The aspects explored are the skills and techniques required to be successful in the game, the environment that skaters skate in, the personal vs. group identity that is shown through the general appearance of the skater, and the values and icons that the game teaches players. We are finding that sport video games support learning; we hope to find how one learns about oneself as a learner from playing.

5. The greatest obstacle to the development of policies for the curtailment of gender bias is lack of information on the scope and effects of the problem. This study represents an attempt to quantify attitudes toward gender bias among profession women engineers working in the State of Kuwait. The major findings that emerged were as follows: a) Since 1970, Kuwait has witnessed an enormous growth rate in the participation of women in higher education. b) With respect to the job-related factors of salary scale, professional treatment, responsibility, benefits, and vacation, a clear majority (68%) of the professional Kuwaiti women engineers surveyed expressed a feeling of equality with or even superiority to their male counterparts. c) The one job-related factor in which significant gender bias was found to be in operation was that of promotion to upper management positions. In this criterion, the women engineers surveyed felt "less than equal" to their male colleagues.

6. The purpose of this study was to determine the status of the health appraisal services provided for primary school children in Edo State, Nigeria. Using the cross-sectional survey design a total of 1506 primary school children were selected from across the state as the study participants. The analysis of data collected through a 14-item questionnaire showed that: four vital aspects of health observation (observation of mouth and teeth, nose and throat, skin, and ears) were not provided for the children; all aspects of health examination were not provided for the children; and records of the health histories of the children were not kept. These results were discussed and the study recommended that professional counselors be enlisted in the schools for a better management of school health services.

Exercise 2

Identify the purpose and theoretical basis, methodology and findings in the following abstract.

The purpose of this research is to find out some main principles, translation strategies and skills to guide Chinese-English (C-E) translation of public signs so that the informative and vocative functions of such texts can be fulfilled. The theoretical basis of this thesis came from Newmark (2001). Newmark points out three main functions of language, namely the expressive, informative and vocative functions, and argues that informative and vocative texts should be communicatively translated. Considering that the chief functions of public signs are informative and vocative, the study concluded that the communicative translation approach should be adopted in translating such texts. This research was based on field corpus study, surveys and qualitative analysis. The author investigated many bilingual public signs and collected a number of them as samples to be critically analyzed. Besides, ten translations of public signs were selected and transcribed for the questionnaire, which was administered to a group of native English speakers to test their communicative effect. The study found out that translators of public signs are inclined to adopt literal translation, neglecting the communicative function of the source text. On the basis of corpus study, the thesis discovered some most common types of translation mistakes. The research also found out that in order to achieve communicative effect, the translation of public signs should conform to the conventions of English public signs, such as shortness in length, plainness in vocabulary and simplicity in sentence structure. The present research is significant in that it yields some important findings regarding the problems existing in the C-E translation of public signs and offers some feasible solutions to these problems.

Unit 9   Introduction for a research paper

9.1   What is the purpose of the introduction?

The introduction comes at the start of a piece of writing. It introduces the research by situating it, presenting the research problem and saying how and why this problem will be "solved". Without this important information the reader cannot easily understand the more detailed information about the research that comes later in the thesis. It also explains why the research is being done (rationale) which is crucial for the reader to understand the significance of the study.

An introduction for a research paper will be quite different from an introduction for an essay. An essay is a more flexible writing form in which writers are often encouraged to be creative in their presentation. Research papers, on the other hand, must be very straightforward and transparent. Therefore, writers of research papers are encouraged to save their creativity for their analysis rather than their introductions.

The first function of the introduction is to define and contextualize the research paper topic. This means that the paper topic should first be thoroughly explained and then contextualized through an explanation of the topic's relevance. For instance, if the research paper were on linguistic ambiguity, the introduction would explain what the linguistic ambiguity is and then give the reason why the linguistic ambiguity is a relevant topic of research. When writing introductions for research papers, students should be sure to fully explain and contextualize, but should stay on track — the explanation and contextualization are only background information for the thesis, which is the main point of the research paper. Therefore, the explanation and contextualization should be thorough, but as concise as possible. The length of the introduction for a research paper will often depend on the complexity of the topic, because more complex topics require more lengthy contextualization and explanation.

After the topic has been explained and contextualized, the writer should present his thesis statement — his main point or argument regarding the research paper topic. The thesis statement follows the explanation and contextualization of the topic because it is only after the topic has been explained and contextualized that a specific argument about that topic can make sense to the reader. This thesis should be clearly articulated in a sentence or group of sentences that assert the research writer's primary point regarding the research paper topic. Often, introductions for research papers end with the assertion of the thesis statement or a sentence or two that explain and contextualize why the thesis is a relevant topic of inquiry.

9.2   What questions will be answered in the introduction?

After reading an introduction, the reader should be able to answer most of these questions.

What is the context of this problem? In what situation or environment can this problem be observed? (Background)

Why is this research important? Who will benefit? Why do we need to know this? Why does this situation, method, model or piece of equipment need to be improved? (Rationale)

What is it we don't know? What is the gap in our knowledge this research will fill? What needs to be improved? (Problem Statement)

What **steps** will the researcher take to try and fill this gap or improve the situation? (Objectives)

Is there any aspect of the problem the researcher will not discuss? Is the study limited to a specific geographical area or to only certain aspects of the situation? (Scope)

Is there any **factor**, **condition** or **circumstance** that prevents the researcher from achieving all his/her objectives? (Limitations)

In considering his/her **method**, model, formulation or approach, does the researcher take certain conditions, states, requirements for granted? Are there certain fundamental conditions or states the researcher takes to be true? (Assumptions)

9.3 How research introductions are organized

The following is the pattern found occurring in many research papers. It is not a set of rules for how you must write — rather, it is a useful guideline for how to think about structuring your information.

1. Establish the field by

claiming centrality (why this field of study is important)

moving from general to specific

reviewing relevant items of previous research

2. Define a research problem by

indicating a gap

raising a question

continuing a previously developed line of inquiry

counter-claiming (disagreeing with an existing/accepted approach)

3. Propose a solution by

outlining purpose/setting objectives

announcing present research (methodology)

announcing principal findings (results)

indicating the structure of the research

9.3.1 Establish the field

First you need to establish the area of research in which your work belongs, and to provide a context for the research problem. This has three main elements.

Claiming centrality: Claiming that the area of research is an important one, and therefore implying that the research done is also crucial. For example: "Minimum safe low temperatures (above freezing) and high humidity control are the most important tools for extending shelf life in vegetables." (Barth et al., 1993). Here the words "the most important tools" indicate centrality by showing that these two factors are crucial.

General to specific: Most writing starts with general information and then moves to specific information. This is true of introductions too.

Previous research: Often the introduction will refer to work already done in the research area in order to provide background (and often also to help define the research problem). For example:

Numerous studies on the utilization of plant proteins as a partial or complete replacement for fish meal in diets have been conducted using various freshwater and marines fishes (Lovell, 1987; Tacon et al., 1983; Murai et al., 1989a; Cowey et al., 1974). (Takii et al., 1989)

9.3.2 Problem

Your research must be new in some way. It must add knowledge *to your field* so you need to show in what way your work explores an area/issue/question that has previously not been explored, or not been explored in detail, in not explored in the way that you are going to use. In other words, you need to give a *rationale* for your work (i.e. show the reasons for doing it). There are four ways to demonstrate that you are adding to the knowledge in your field:

Gap: A research gap is an area where no or little research has been carried out. This is shown by outlining the work *already* done to show where there is a gap in the research. For example:

Numerous studies on the utilization of plant proteins as a partial or complete replacement for fish meal in diets have been conducted using various freshwater and marines fishes (Lovell, 1987; Tacon et al., 1983; Murai et al., 1989a; Cowey et al., 1974). However, very little is known about the feasibility of using soybean meal as a dietary protein source in practical feeds for yellowtail Seriola quinqueradiata. (Takii et al., 1989)

Raising a question: The research problem is defined by asking a question to which the answer is unknown, and which you will explore in your research. For example:

The question we address here is how technological change occurs when it is the overall system that needs to be changed. In particular, how can we begin and sustain a technological transition away from hydrocarbon based technologies? (Street and Miles, 1996)

Continuing a previously developed line of enquiry: Building on work already done, but taking it further (by using a new sample, extending the area studied, taking more factors into consideration, taking fewer factors into consideration, etc.).

Counter-claiming: A conflicting claim, theory or method is put forward.

9.3.3 Solution

Once the field and problem have been defined, it is time to give the "solution." In other words, how will the research gap be filled? How will the question that was raised be answered? This last part of the introduction can also be used to show the benefits, to explain the objectives, to clarify the scope of the research, to announce what was found from doing the research and how it can be used. Notice that an introduction will discuss a number of the following points but is unlikely to cover them all.

Outlining purpose: Often researchers will describe their objectives in their introduction in order for the reader to have a clear idea of what they set out to accomplish. Usually there is a general objective written in one sentence.

Announcing present research (method): Important points about the methodology used are outlined, perhaps including the scope of the study. However, the methodology is *not* given in detail (since details are given in the methodology section). For example:

This paper examines the use of peat for the removal of two metals, copper and nickel, from both mono-solute and bi-solute solutions. In particular, it reports the effect that a competing ion has on the rates of removal and examines the mechanisms which may affect the uptake of minerals. (Ho et al., 1996)

Announcing principle findings (results): Researchers may indicate the kind of results they obtained, or an overall summary of their findings.

Indicating the structure of the research: It is useful to outline the organization of the written up research that follows so that the reader has a clear idea of what is going to follow, and in what order.

Indicating directions for further research: Research often opens up other areas where research could or should be done, so it is common for these areas to be defined in the introduction. It is also a way of indicating that the current study is not designed to be comprehensive.

Indicating benefits of current research: Indicating the benefits of the research helps to justify why it was carried out and emphasizes the value of the study.

9.4 Language used in the introduction

Phrases which are commonly employed in the introductions are listed below.
Establishing the importance of the topic:
One of the most significant current discussions in language learning is...
It is becoming increasingly difficult to ignore the...
In the new global economy, X has become a central issue for...
In the history of development economics, X has been thought of as a key factor in...
Establishing the importance of the topic (time frame given):
In recent years, there has been an increasing interest in...

Recently, researchers have shown an increased interest in...

The past decade has seen the rapid development of X in many...

Over the past century there has been a dramatic increase in...

Highlighting a problem or controversy in the field of study:

However, these rapid changes are having a serious effect...

However, a major problem with this kind of application is...

To date there has been little agreement on what...

Highlighting a knowledge gap in the field of study (for research):

So far, however, there has been little discussion about...

However, far too little attention has been paid to...

However, there have been no controlled studies which compare differences in...

The experimental data are rather controversial, and there is no general agreement about...

Focus and aim:

This paper will focus on/examine/give an account of...

This paper seeks to address the following questions:

This essay critically examines/discusses/traces...

This paper will review the research conducted on...

This chapter reviews the literature concerning the usefulness of using...

The aim of this paper is to determine/examine...

Outline of structure:

This paper has been divided into four parts. The first part deals with...

The essay has been organised in the following way.

This paper first gives a brief overview of the recent history of X.

This paper begins by... It will then go on to...

The first section of this paper will examine...

Explaining keywords

While a variety of definitions of the term X have been suggested, this paper will use the definition first suggested by Smith (1968) who saw it as...

Throughout this paper the term X will refer to/will be used to refer to...

In this article the acronym/abbreviation XYZ will be used.

9.5 Summary

To sum up, the introduction for a research paper is the beginning section of the paper that contextualizes the **research paper topic** and articulates the paper's thesis. All **research paper introductions** should contain information that allows the reader to fully understand the paper topic, the topic's relevance, and the paper's thesis before proceeding to more in-depth examination or exploration.

There are many ways to introduce an academic paper. Most academic writers, however, appear to do one or more of the following in their introductions:

- establish the context, background and/or importance of the topic
- indicate a problem, controversy or a gap in the field of study
- define the topic or key terms
- state of the purpose of the essay/writing
- provide an overview of the coverage and/or structure of the writing

Exercise 1

Identify what the writer does in the following sample introduction.
Introduction

Many commentators have noted that sentence connectors (e. g., however) are an important and useful element in expository and argumentative writing. Frequency studies of their occurrence in academic English extend at least as far back as Huddleston (1971). ESL writing textbooks have for many years regularly included chapters on sentence connectors (e. g. Herber, 1965). Most reference grammars deal with their grammatical status, classification, meaning, and use. Some attention has also been given to the position of sentence connectors in clauses and sentences. Quirk and Greenbaum (1973) observe (a) that the normal position is initial; (b) that certain connectors, such as hence and overall, "are restricted, or virtual restricted, to initial position" (p. 248); and (c) that medial positions are rare for most connectors, and final positions even rarer. The only attempt known to us to explain differences in position on semantic grounds is an unpublished paper by Salera (1976) discussed by Celce-Murcia and Larsen-Freeman (1983). The Salera paper deals only with adversatives like *however* and suggests that initial position reflects something contrary to expectation, while medial position reflects a contract that is not necessarily unexpected. However, neither of these studies provides any descriptive evidence of the actual positions of sentence connectors in academic texts. In the present paper, we report on a preliminary study of sentence connector position in a sample of twelve published articles.

Exercise 2

Take one of the phrases below and use it to write a sentence stating the importance of research you are currently conducting or have conducted in the past.

Recently, there has been growing interest in...

The possibility of... has generated wide interest in...

The development of... is a classic problem in...

The... has become a favorite topic for analysis...

Knowledge of... has a great importance for...

The study of... has become an important aspect of...

A central issue in... is...

The... has been extensively studied in recent years.

Many investigators have recently turned to...

The relationship between... has been investigated by many researchers.

Many recent studies have focused on...

Exercise 3

Write a negative statement about the research you are reviewing for your final project using the format below.

Verbs

However, previous research in this field has _____.

_____ a. concentrated on x.   _____ g. neglected to consider x.
_____ b. disregarded x.   _____ h. overestimated x.
_____ c. failed to consider x.   _____ i. overlooked x.
_____ d. ignored x.   _____ j. been restricted to x.
_____ e. been limited to x.   _____ k. suffered from x.
_____ f. misinterpreted x.   _____ l. underestimated x.

Adjectives

Nevertheless, these attempts to establish a link between secondary smoke and lung cancer are at present _____.

_____ a. controversial   _____ e. questionable
_____ b. incomplete   _____ f. unconvincing
_____ c. inconclusive   _____ g. unsatisfactory
_____ d. misguided

Exercise 4

Use one of the following sentences to introduce what you will do in your research paper.

1. The aim of the present paper is to give...
2. This paper reports on the results obtained...
3. In this paper we give preliminary results for...
4. The main purpose of the experiment reported here was to...
5. This study was designed to evaluate...
6. The present work extends the use of the last model by...
7. We now report the interaction between....
8. The primary focus of this paper is on...
9. The aim of this investigation was to test...
10. It is the purpose of the present paper to provide...

Exercise 5

Study the following sample introduction carefully to identify the patterns you have learned in 9.3 in this unit.

Stereotypes abound in today's society. People seem to have an innate compulsion to categorise others into various groups and then to apply rigid and limited descriptions to these groups. There are therefore, amongst others, stereotypical nationalities and races; stereotypical sexes and sexual orientations and stereotypical classes. And one place where these stereotypes often thrive is in the mass media, particularly in the tabloid press and popular television, such as in situation comedy. Some, for example Hick (1996), claim that this is a harmless phenomenon, whereas commentators such as Ealham (1998) point to the possible dangers of obsessive stereotyping in the media. This essay will examine what sociological evidence there is for the process of stereotyping in the mass media, and will then go on to analyse the reasons for its occurrence. The final part of the essay will ask how far society's attitudes are in fact shaped by this portrayal of the various kinds of stereotypes.

Unit 10 Writing a literature review

10.1 What is a literature review?

A literature review is a survey and discussion of the literature in a given area of study. It is a concise overview of what has been studied, argued, and established about a topic, and it is usually organized chronologically or thematically. A literature review is written in essay format. It is not an annotated bibliography, because it groups related works together and discusses trends and developments rather than focusing on one item at a time. It is not a summary; rather, it evaluates previous and current research in regard to how relevant and/or useful it is and how it relates to your own research.

There are two main approaches to a literature review. One approach is to choose an area of research, read all the relevant studies, and organize them in a meaningful way. An example of an organizing theme is a conflict or controversy in the area, where you might first discuss the studies that support one side, then discuss the studies that support the other side. Another approach is to choose an organizing theme or a point that you want to make, then select your studies accordingly.

Regardless of how you decide to organize your literature review, it will have two purposes: ① to thoroughly describe work done on a specific area of research, ② to evaluate this work. Both the descriptive and evaluative elements are important parts of the review. You can't do one or the other. If you just describe past research without evaluating it, you are merely summarizing information without digesting it. If you just discuss recent theories in an area without describing the work done to test those theories, then your arguments lack supporting empirical evidence.

Authors of literature reviews evaluate a body of literature by identifying relations, contradictions, gaps, and inconsistencies in the literature and by suggesting the next step needed to solve the research problem. A literature review may compare studies in terms of assumptions about the research question, experimental method, data analysis, and any conclusions drawn.

10.2 Purpose

A literature review is written to highlight specific arguments and ideas in a field of study. By highlighting these arguments, the writer attempts to show what has been studied in the field, and also where the weaknesses, gaps, or areas needing further study are. The review should therefore also demonstrate to the reader why the writer's research is useful, necessary, important, and valid.

10.3 Reasons for writing a literature review

Literature reviews provide you with a handy guide to a particular topic. If you have limited time to conduct research, literature reviews can give you an overview or act as a stepping stone. For professionals, they are useful reports that keep them up to date with what is current in the field. For scholars, the depth and breadth of the literature review emphasizes the credibility of the writer in his or her field. Literature reviews also provide a solid background for a research paper's investigation. Comprehensive knowledge of the literature of the field is essential to most research papers.

Specifically, literature reviews can help you in the following aspects.

Identify a testable hypothesis

Once you have identified a broad problem area — practical or theoretical — the next step is to review the literature on the topic. Examining both the theoretical and research literature on a topic usually will help you narrow your topic and identify a testable hypothesis.

Identifying measuring tools (instruments)

You may identify instruments that were used successfully by other researchers and, also, avoid those found to be seriously flawed.

Avoid dead-ends

Your research idea may have already been thoroughly investigated and shown to be not useful.

Aids in writing research reports

Paying careful attention to the style and organization used by authors of published research, you will learn about organization and structure of written reports.

Helps with citations

If you are researching in a Sociological or Social Science journal or article, you can gain useful information regarding the proper format for citations in your area of study.

Demonstrate relevance of your hypothesis

A proper literature review enables you to show those who are reviewing your research that you were able to locate research relevant to your hypothesis, to use it in planning your research, and to cite it appropriately in your review of literature.

10.4 Questions a literature review should answer

Asking questions such as the following will help you sift through your sources and organize your literature review. Remember, the literature review organizes the previous research in the light of what you are planning to do in your own project.

What's been done in this topic area to date? What are the significant discoveries, key concepts, arguments, and/or theories that scholars have put forward? Which are the important works?

On which particular areas of the topic has previous research concentrated? Have there been developments over time? What methodologies have been used?

Are there any gaps in the research? Are there areas that haven't been looked at closely yet, but which should be? Are there new ways of looking at the topic?

Are there improved methodologies for researching this subject?

What future directions should research in this subject take?

How will your research build on or depart from current and previous research on the topic? What contribution will your research make to the field?

10.5 Structure of a literature review

There are several ways to organize and structure a literature review. Three common ways are chronologically and thematically and methodologically.

Chronological: In a chronological review, you will group and discuss your sources in order of their appearance (usually publication), highlighting the changes in research in the field and your specific topic over time.

Thematic: In a thematic review, you will group and discuss your sources in terms of the themes or topics they cover. This method is often a stronger one organizationally, and it can help you resist the urge to summarize your sources. By grouping themes or topics of research together, you will be able to demonstrate the types of topics that are important to your research.

Methodological: A methodological approach differs from the two above in that the focusing factor usually does not have to do with the content of the material. Instead, it focuses on the "methods" of the researcher or writer.

Within each section of a literature review, it is important to discuss how the research relates to other studies (how is it similar or different, what other studies have been done, etc.) as well as to demonstrate how it relates to your own work. This is what the review is for: don't leave this connection out.

10.6 Steps in writing literature review

There are four main steps in writing a literature review: ① find a focus, ② read the relevant articles, ③ work out a thesis statement, ④ consider the organization of the review and ⑤ write the review. Each step is discussed in more detail below.

10.6.1 Find a focus

A literature review, like a term paper, is usually organized around ideas, not the sources themselves. This means that you will not just simply list your sources and go into detail about each one of them, one at a time. As you read widely but selectively in your topic area, consider instead what themes or issues connect your sources together. Pick one of these themes to focus the organization of your review.

10.6.2 Read the articles

Reading research articles is different from other types of reading. It tends to be slow and sometimes frustrating if you are not familiar with the topic and the language of the field. A good understanding of the research literature is a necessary prerequisite for writing a competent review article yourself. Understanding the literature requires you to read, re-read, and mentally digest complex ideas.

10.6.3 Construct a working thesis statement

Once you have finished reading the relevant article, you can use the ideas you've found to construct a thesis statement. Literature reviews have thesis statements as well. However, your thesis statement will not necessarily argue for a position or an opinion; rather it will argue for a particular perspective on the material.

10.6.4 Consider organization

You've got a focus, and you've narrowed it down to a thesis statement. Now what is the most effective way of presenting the information? What are the most important topics, subtopics, etc., that your review needs to include? And in what order should you present them? To help you come up with an overall organizational framework for your review, consider the following three typical ways of organizing the sources into a review: *chronological*, *thematic*, *and methodological.* (refer to 9.5 for more detailed discussions of these three approaches)

Once you've decided on the organizational method for the body of the review, the sections you need to include in the paper should be easy to figure out. They should arise out of your organizational strategy. In other words, a chronological review would have subsections for each vital time period. A thematic review would have subtopics based upon factors that relate to the theme or issue.

10.6.5 Writing the review

Once you've settled on a general pattern of organization, you're ready to write the review. There are a few guidelines you should follow during the writing stage. Here is a sample paragraph from a literature review about sexism and language to illuminate the following discussion.

However, other studies have shown that even gender-neutral antecedents are more likely to produce masculine images than feminine ones (Gastil, 1990). Hamilton (1988) asked students to complete sentences that required them to fill in pronouns that agreed with gender-neutral antecedents such as "writer", "pedestrian", and "persons". The students were asked to describe any image they had when writing the sentence. Hamilton found that people imagined 3.3 men to each woman in the masculine "generic" condition and 1.5 men per woman in the unbiased condition. Thus, while ambient sexism accounted for some of the masculine bias, sexist language amplified the effect.

Use evidence

In the example above, the writers refer to several other sources when making their point. A literature review in this sense is just like any other academic research paper. Your interpretation of the available sources must be backed up with evidence to show that what you are saying is valid.

Be selective

Select only the most important points in each source to highlight in the review. The type of information you choose to mention should relate directly to the review's focus, whether it is thematic, methodological, or chronological.

Use quotes sparingly

Falk and Mills do not use any direct quotes. That is because the survey nature of the literature review does not allow for in-depth discussion or detailed quotes from the text. Some short quotes here and there are okay, though, if you want to emphasize a point, or if what the author said just cannot be rewritten in your own words. Notice that Falk and Mills do quote certain terms that were coined by the author, not common knowledge, or taken directly from the study. But if you find yourself wanting to put in more quotes, check with your instructor.

Summarize and synthesize

Remember to summarize and synthesize your sources within each paragraph as well as throughout the review. The authors here recapitulate important features of Hamilton's study, but then synthesize it by rephrasing the study's significance and relating it to their own work.

Keep your own voice

While the literature review presents others' ideas, your voice (the writer's) should remain front and center. Notice that Falk and Mills weave references to other sources into their own text, but they still maintain their own voice by starting and ending the paragraph with their own ideas and their own words. The sources support what Falk and Mills are saying.

Use caution when paraphrasing

When paraphrasing a source that is not your own, be sure to represent the author's information or opinions accurately and in your own words. In the preceding example, Falk and Mills either directly refer in the text to the author of their source, such as Hamilton, or they provide ample notation in the text when the ideas they are mentioning are not their own, for example, Gastil's.

10.7 Examples

Example 1

This chapter will briefly review specific factors that are relevant to educational aspirations and/or deviant behavior. Researchers as well as theorists continue to strive for answers to such questions as, Who are juvenile delinquents? Are there special characteristics associated with delinquents? Do delinquents vary among themselves; and if so, How do they differ? Although multiple predictive variables tend to reoccur throughout much of the research, many theorists do acknowledge that not any one variable, or theory, exclusively explains all of delinquent behavior. Using several current studies of delinquency, we will discuss common social factors that are associated with delinquent behavior: Social structural factors include age, gender, and ethnicity; social bond factors include school, family, economics, and religion; and the social psychological factor includes purpose of life.

Social Structural Factors

Age

*One of the strongest, but not inclusive, variables used to explain delinquent behavior is that of age. When Gottfredson and Hirschi (1986) examined all offenders, they found that the relationship between crime and age is such that the tendency to commit criminal acts reaches a peak in the middle to late teens and then declines rapidly throughout life (U. S. Department of Justice, 1985b: 346). Furthermore, based on data sources from England, Wales, France and the United States over the past 150 years, they (1985) contend that: ① the frequency of criminal acts rapidly rise through the teen years, ② twenty years old is the age at which criminal behavior peaks. (**This continues through all social structural factors**)...*

Social Bond Factors

...Within the life-course tradition, Moffitt (1993) theorizes that the ALs develop "strong attachments to work and family for the same reason they desist from delinquency: Youthful delinquency followed by adult bonding to work and family constitute a sequence of normal developmental stages (for males)." Furthermore, other research of criminal behavior suggests the same conclusion of maturation (see Empey and Erickson, 1972; Murray and Cox, 1979). Gottfredson and Hirschi argue that "maturational reform is so pervasively observed, even among serious delinquents that it is the dominant explanation of change in criminal activity during the teen years" (1986: 221)...

Example 2

...The connection between crime and substance abuse is well documented, but nowhere is it more obvious than in data on recidivism rates. Statistics show that the more prior convictions an individual has, the more likely it is that the individual is a drug or alcohol abuser (Belenko & Peugh, 1998). Among state prison populations, 41 percent of first offenders are regular substance users, compared with 63 percent of inmates who have two prior convictions and 81 percent of those who have five or more convictions. Some 39 percent of regular substance users in state prisons have two or more prior incarcerations, compared with only 21 percent of state inmates who are not regular substance users (Belenko & Peugh, 1998).

Another contributing factor to prison overcrowding is "get tough" policies that can range from tougher laws such as Three Strikes laws to mandatory sentencing for specific crimes. In many states, most notably California (Vitello, 1997), Three Strikes laws have been established to give judges and/or prosecutors more sentencing power when dealing with repeat offenders. Some states have a type of graduated scale for implementation of

Three Strikes laws, in that the second felony conviction can net an offender a sentence which is double that of the recommended sentence of a first conviction (Vitello, 1997). Typically, a third felony conviction can, and often does, land a repeat offender in prison for life. These longer sentences and mandatory life sentences can have a definite effect on prison populations for years to come.

It is difficult to talk about "get tough" policies without going back to the issue of drug abuse. For years, federal, state and local officials have consistently stepped up law enforcement, prosecution and punishment in response to citizen concerns about crime and violence (CASA 1998). Beginning with the heroin epidemic of the 1970's and continuing through the crack-cocaine explosion in the 1980's...

Example 3

Much of the research discussed the role of women in the Catholic Church since it is a current topic of controversy within the faith. Other articles examined and discussed the roles of women in various Protestant faiths. These topics will be dealt with in a later section of the literature review. Importantly, one of the articles, "Gender and Religious Work" (Heyer-Gray 2000) went beyond an explanation of the roles of women and dealt with why the role of women in the church is an important topic. The author of the article, Heyer-Gray, examined the roles of women in the church as related to feminism and how the roles of women within a larger framework are devalued. This is a very important topic to consider since according to Michael Kimmel, gender is "... one of the primary axes around which social life is organized" (Kimmel 1993 : vii). Heyer-Gray examined how religious work is "gendered" and how it is important in discussions of the goals of feminist movements (2000).

Heyer-Gray, highlighted three key feminist themes that she felt were areas of concern in the roles of women in various churches (2000). Her first concern was "... rendering visible those kinds of work that in fact sustain our everyday worlds — our households, our communities, our churches — but that are often difficult to 'see' or discern even occasionally for those who actually do the work" (Heyer-Gray 2000)...

Exercise 1

Here is an example of a literature review on the subject of *Language & Gender*.
Work out the *sequence* to his review and the *sources* the writer uses.

Language and gender: A brief Literature Review

With the general growth of feminist work in many academic fields, it is hardly surprising that the relationship between language and gender has attracted considerable attention in recent years. In an attempt to go beyond "folklinguistic" assumptions about how men and women use language (the assumption that women are "talkative", for example), studies have focused on anything from different syntactical, phonological or lexical uses of language to aspects of conversation analysis, such as topic nomination and control, interruptions and other interactional features. While some research has focused only on the description of differences, other work has sought to show how linguistic differences both reflect and reproduce social difference. Accordingly, Coates (1988) suggests that research on language and gender can be divided into studies that focus on dominance and those that focus on difference.

Much of the earlier work emphasized dominance. Lakoff's (1975) pioneering work suggested that women's speech typically displayed a range of features, such as tag questions, which marked it as inferior and weak. Thus, she argued that the type of subordinate speech learned by a young girl "will later be an excuse others use to keep her in a demeaning position, to refuse to treat her seriously as a human being" (1975, p. 5). While there are clearly some problems with Lakoff's work — her analysis was not based on empirical research, for example, and the automatic equation of subordinate with 'weak' is problematic — the emphasis on dominance has understandably remained at the Centre of much of this work. Research has shown how men nominated topics more, interrupted more often, held the floor for longer, and so on (see, for example, Zimmerman and West, 1975). The chief focus of this approach, then, has been to show how patterns of interaction between men and women reflect the dominant position of men in society.

Some studies, however, have taken a different approach by looking not so much at power in mixed-sex interactions as at how same-sex groups produce certain types of interaction. In a typical study of this type, Maltz and Borker (1982) developed lists of what they described as men's and women's features of language. They argued that these norms of interaction were acquired in same-sex groups rather than mixed-sex groups and that the issue is therefore one of (sub-) cultural miscommunication rather than social inequality. Much of this research has focused on comparisons between, for example, the competitive conversational style of men and the cooperative conversational style of women.

While some of the more popular work of this type, such as Tannen (1987), lacks a critical dimension, the emphasis on difference has nevertheless been valuable in fostering research into gender subgroup interactions and in emphasizing the need to see women's language use not only as "subordinate" but also as a significant subcultural domain.

Although Coates' (1988) distinction is clearly a useful one, it also seems evident that these two approaches are by no means mutually exclusive. While it is important on the one hand, therefore, not to operate with a simplistic version of power and to consider language and gender only in mixed-group dynamics, it is also important not to treat women's linguistic behaviour as if it existed outside social relations of power. As Cameron, McAlinden and O'Leary (1988) ask, "Can it be coincidence that men are aggressive and hierarchically-organized conversationalists, whereas women are expected to provide conversational support?" (p. 80). Clearly, there is scope here for a great deal more research that

- is based on empirical data of men's and women's speech;
- operates with a complex understanding of power and gender relationships (so that

women's silence, for example, can be seen both as a site of oppression and as a site of possible resistance);
- looks specifically at the contexts of language use, rather than assuming broad gendered differences;
- involves more work by men on language and gender, since attempts to understand male uses of language in terms of difference have been few (thus running the danger of constructing men's speech as the "norm" and women's speech as "different");
- aims not only to describe and explain but also to change language and social relationships.

Unit 11　Conclusion

11.1　What is a conclusion and what is its purpose?

The conclusion is the last part that your reader will read, so it is what you use to make your final impression on your reader. The conclusion is the final place to convey to your reader the quality of your paper — both in terms of writing style and content. Just as you want your first impression in your paper to be a good one, you want your final impression to be equally good. You'll have some decisions to make so your conclusion is an invaluable part of your paper.

The conclusion of the research paper is the most valuable single part of it. All the material you have gathered means nothing to your reader until you present the conclusion you have reached as a result of your research. Restate your thesis and show what the material you have presented adds up to. Analyze and evaluate your main points for your reader; also consider the consequences and general implications of them to your conclusion. Although no actual new information is usually introduced in the concluding paragraphs, the conclusion is the only "original" contribution you offer in your paper. It manifests the value of your research as well as your understanding of the material that you have presented. It should be a strong recapitulation of your major ideas.

There are several purposes of a conclusion. The most obvious is to explain the whole paper and answer the most primary research paper question that was thought before creating the paper or in general terms, it will answer the direct question of the research paper. The conclusion also evaluates the significance of the paper, reemphasizes the main points, predicts an outcome, offers a solution, or suggests a further study.

A good conclusion should be more than just a summary. It should be a thoughtful end to a piece of writing; for example, by applying what you have written to the outside world. A good conclusion should emphasize or reinforce your main ideas, but with your ideas restated in a fresh way: don't use the same language again. You should refer back to your introduction, either with key words or parallel concepts and images.

A good conclusion can suggest results or consequences or make a call for some sort of action. It can make predictions or suggest solutions.

11.2　What should you do when writing a conclusion?

In your conclusion you have the opportunity to strengthen your essay by bringing logical closure to the full scope of your ideas. When writing a conclusion one must remember that the reader is trying to grasp what they have just read and make a final opinion about it. Therefore, you must summarize the points you made in the paper to refresh the reader's mind. You can achieve this purpose by using the following strategies.

— Summarize the main points of the paper.

— Turn the discussion back to something you mentioned in your introduction.

— Look ahead to the future.

— Address ideas from a fresh perspective in order to encourage the reader to continue thinking about your topic.

— Save a provocative, unexpected, or exciting insight or quotation for the conclusion.

11.3 Things to avoid in the conclusion

We have looked at several strategies concerning how to end the research paper. But, there are a few that you should avoid doing in your conclusion.

(1) Don't apologize for your paper.

(2) Don't bring up completely new ideas.

(3) Don't change the tone or style of your writing.

(4) Don't contradict your thesis or any part of your paper.

(5) Don't make exaggerated claims.

(6) Don't restate the introduction word for word.

11.4 Sample conclusions

Example

It has been shown, therefore, that stereotypes have always existed in society, and probably will always do so. The mass media is a relatively recent phenomenon, which is one reason for the widely differing views on its role in creating and fostering stereotypical images. The actual causes of stereotyping in the mass media have been shown to be surprisingly diverse, although there can be no argument that any form of it which leads, albeit indirectly, to suffering in any form must not be allowed to take place. It is society itself which must stop this from happening, as laws and regulations are often ineffective. Things are changing, though, and in some areas very quickly; some commonplace stereotypes of only twenty years ago and today virtually taboo. It is society which must indirectly control the mass media, not vice versa. However, in an increasingly "global" world, controlled by fewer and fewer corporations and individuals eager to please the governments of the major world powers, and, in the mass media, who are more than willing to use stereotyping as a tool in the control of society, we must be more and more vigilant to avoid this cynical manipulation.

Exercise 1

Write a conclusion to match each of the following introductions.

Introduction 1

In one minute, 100 football fields of the rainforest are gone. Deforestation is the process of cutting down trees, killing animals or plants, and ruining the natural habitat of the rainforest. The biggest cause of deforestation is logging. There are many other causes as well as adjusting to overpopulation by constructing houses or buildings. The need for goods, such as rubber for tires, is also a reason for deforestation. Humans are affected because the whole world suffers when the rainforest is destroyed. The climate changes and the air gets warmer when trees are cut or burned down. Although the problem of rainforest destruction continues, people are currently trying to stop it. Organizations such as the World Wildlife Fund have set up reserves for animals and plants where they can live safely. Colobine monkeys are in danger from the destruction because they spend half their time in trees and the trees are rapidly being cut down.

Introduction 2

"Unseen they suffer, unheard they cry, in the loneliness they linger, in the darkness they die," is a quote from the People for the Ethical Treatment of Animals. Each month, millions of animals suffer and die because of the testing of toxic products and weapons on animals. The cruelty of animal testing causes many animals to die horrible, painful deaths, even though they didn't do anything to deserve this fate. Why do we test products on animals, when we wouldn't want these products tested on ourselves? There are many reasons why animal testing is wrong and should be stopped.

Exercise 2

The following paragraph below has lost its conclusion. Write a sentence that would help the reader to look back at the whole scene that the writer has described.

A stream in one of our state parks has always been my sitting spot. I am fascinated when I see the water bubbling over and down the rocks. The water has shaped the rocks, causing deep indentations in certain places, but other parts are perfectly flat. The rocks seem to be lined up in descending order so that the water flows evenly in every direction, making white foam. The sound of the water rushing under the bridge always grabs my attention and sends chills up my spine. On the other side of the bridge is a pond full of fish. Nearby there is a place where people can go swimming or just sit on the bank and relax in the sand. Beyond that is a long bicycle path which leads behind some tall trees, and there are picnic areas along with grills and tables.

Exercise 3

The essay below has lost its conclusion. Add a final paragraph as the conclusion
Relief

Relief is a feeling that comes when a great weight has been lifted from your shoulders. Whatever burden you felt is magically gone. When you are finally released from whatever problem you had, your inner self is at peace, because you no longer have to worry. Imagine this example: You are carrying a heavy rock up a steep hill. When you finally get to the top of that hill you are happy because you can put your load down. That is what relief feels like.

Childbirth is very complex because of the many emotions you feel at the same time. I think the biggest emotion I felt when Shane was born was relief. When I carried my baby for 9 months, the doctor told me everything was all right through his examinations. I didn't believe him. I worried that Shane might be born with some type of defect or he would be stillborn. I couldn't wait for his birth so I could see for myself. I think I worried so much that I made myself sick. I was always running to the doctor asking, "What does this symptom mean?" When Shane was finally born I counted his tiny fingers and toes, checked to see that he had a tongue, and in fact that he was a boy. Finally the worrying was over and I could see for myself that I had a perfect angel. Now I could enjoy my bundle.

Unit 12 Summary

12.1 Reasons for writing summaries

Although the papers you write will be your own — your own voice, your own thesis statements — there will be times when you will want to integrate source material to help you support your assertions. If your purpose is one of the following, you may wish to summarize a whole text or a portion of a text:

to discuss someone's argument or text directly;
to supply context for a specific point in another's text that you are discussing;
to use as expert evidence for a point you are making in your own argumentative text;
to present an opposing point of view that you wish to refute.

12.2 Definition of summary

A summary is a shortened version of another's text, explanation, argument, or narrative. It includes all of the main points of the original but reduces the detail of the original.

In another word, the summary is a brief restatement of the content of a passage (a group of paragraphs, a chapter, an article, or a book). This restatement should focus on the *central idea* of the passage. A summary may be as brief as one or two sentences (the central idea only) or one paragraph (the central idea and its supporting points), or as lengthy as several paragraphs (the central idea, its supporting points, and some important examples), depending on its purpose. In addition, it will not contain any of the student's opinions. A good summary should be brief, complete, and objective.

One of the more difficult aspects of writing a summary is maintaining objectivity. A student should strive to be as objective as possible when summarizing. The level of objectivity achieved, however, may vary depending on the student's background, experience, and knowledge of the piece being summarized. Although restating a central idea and the main points might sound like a simple task, a student may have something in his or her background that biases his or her summary of an article. A student may not have any knowledge of an article's subject matter, which could affect his or her ability to distinguish the most important points of a piece. Remaining objective can be difficult for students, but practice at writing summaries will improve their ability to do so.

12.3 Preparations

First of all, you should read the text and make notes of the most important facts.
- Examine the context.
- Note the title and subtitle.
- Identify the main point.

- Identify the subordinate points.
- Break the reading into sections.
- Distinguish between points, examples, and counterarguments.
- Watch for transitions within and between paragraphs.
- Read actively and recursively.

12.4 How to write summaries

- Write one-sentence summaries of each stage of thought.
- Write a one- or two-sentence summary of the entire passage.
- Write the first draft of your summary.
- Check your summary against the original passage.
- Revise your summary.

Look at the following passage.

Height connotes status in many parts of the world. Executive offices are usually on the top floors; the underlings work below. Even being tall can help a person succeed. Studies have shown that employers are more willing to hire men over 6 feet tall than shorter men with the same credentials. Studies of real-world executives and graduates have shown that taller men make more money. In one study, every extra inch of height brought in an extra $1 300 a year. But being too big can be a disadvantage. A tall, brawny football player complained that people found him intimidating off the field and assumed he "had the brains of a Twinkie." (p. 301)

Let's first identify the main points in the original passage.

Topic sentence: Height connotes status in many parts of the world.

Main point: Even being tall can help a person succeed.

Main point: Executive offices are usually on the top.

Main point: Being too big can be a disadvantage.

Then we may put all the ideas together to create the following summary of the original passage.

Though height may connote slowness to some people, in the business world, it is almost universally associated with success. For example, taller men are more likely to be hired and to have greater salaries. Further, those in top positions within a company are more likely to work on the top floors of office buildings (Locker, 2003).

12.5 How to include summaries in your text

Introduce the topic in your own words, but make it clear that you are presenting someone else's ideas with wording like "H. H. Smith argues that..." or "According to medical researcher Donald Smith,..." or "Smith also claims that...".

A good way to make sure you've completely represented the author's ideas is to write down something for each paragraph of the original text. Then delete any ideas that don't seem to be central to the argument. One example of this might be a full paragraph that develops one particular illustration of the point the author is making; your summary would include the point but not the illustration.

Make sure that you've gotten the main idea of each paragraph. If the author consistently uses topic sentences, use them as clues to the structure of his or her argument as a whole. Remember that a topic sentence can appear anywhere in a paragraph — beginning, middle, or end.

Present the ideas of the original using your own sentence structure as well as your own word choice.

Cite your source, even if you do not use a direct quotation from the source.

First, look at this passage.

Today, pornography attempts to make its audience focus their fantasies on specific people. The "Playmate of the Month" is a particular woman about whom the reader is meant to have particular fantasies. In my view, this has a more baneful effect on people — makes them demented, in fact, in a way that earlier pornography didn't. Today's pornography promises them that there exists, somewhere on this earth, a life of endlessly desirable and available women and endlessly potent men. The promise that this life is just around the corner — in Hugh Hefner's mansion, or even just in the next joint or the next snort — is maddening and disorienting. And in its futility, it makes for rage and self-hatred. The traditional argument against censorship — that "no one can be seduced by a book" — was probably valid when pornography was impersonal and anonymous, purely an aid to fantasizing about sexual utopia. Today, however, there is addiction and seduction in pornography.

From: Decter, M. (1998) The Growth of Pornography in Society London: Raymonde Press

If you have read the above passage and would like to include a summary of it in your paper, you can do it like this.

Decter (1998) argues that because pornography is more realistic now, using photographs of people with names and identities, it is more harmful to its readers and viewers, who can easily grow dissatisfied and frustrated with fantasies.

12.6 Examples

Original source

In some respects, the increasing frequency of mountain lion encounters in California has as much to do with a growing human population as it does with rising mountain lion numbers. The scenic solitude of the western ranges is prime cougar habitat, and it is falling swiftly to the developer's spade. Meanwhile, with their ideal habitat already at its carrying capacity, mountain lions are forcing younger cats into less suitable terrain, including residential areas. Add that cougars have generally grown bolder under a lengthy ban on their being hunted, and an unsettling scenario begins to emerge.

Summary

Encounters between mountain lions and humans are on the rise in California because increasing numbers of lions are competing for a shrinking habitat. As the lions' wild habitat shrinks, older lions force younger lions into residential areas. These lions have lost some of their fear of humans because of a ban on hunting.

Exercise 1

Read the following passages. Then, including only the main idea and the primary supporting detail, compose a one-sentence general summary statement and then a one-sentence specific summary statement.

Example

The dining table is covered with a white cloth. The maid has laid the table in the usual way and has put the right number of knives, forks, spoons and glasses for each person. There is also pepper and salt, oil and vinegar and mustard. On the left of each person is a table-napkin and a plate with a roll on it. In front of the host there is a carving knife and fork.

A general summary:

The table was laid for dinner.

A specific summary:

The table was laid for dinner with enough tableware for each person and condiment and other things needed.

Paragraph 1

The neurotic individual may have had some special vulnerability as an infant. Perhaps he was ill a great deal and was given care that singled him out Tom other children. Perhaps he walked or talked much later — or earlier than children were expected to, and this evoked unusual treatment. The child whose misshapen feet must be put in casts or the sickly little boy who never can play ball may get out of step with his age mates and with the expectations parents and other adults have about children. Or a child may be very unusually placed in his family. He may be the only boy with six sisters, or a tiny child between two lusty sets of twins or the source of the child's difficulties may be a series of events that deeply affected his relations to people — the death of his mother at the birth of the next child or the prolonged illness or absence of his father. Or a series of coincidences — an accident to a parent, moving to a new town and a severe fright — taken together may alter a child's relationship with the world.

Paragraph 2

Suppose you fly in a plane. What is more important for you: the pilot's real competence or his papers that certify he is competent? Or suppose you get sick and need medical treatment. What is more important for you: your doctor's real competence or his diploma? Of course, in every case the real competence is more important. But last year I met a large group of people whose priorities were exactly the opposite: my students. Not all, but many. Their first priority was to get papers that certify that they are competent rather than to develop real competence. As soon as I started to explain to them something that was a little bit beyond the standard courses, they asked suspiciously: "Will this be on the test?" If I said "no," they did not listen any more and showed clearly that I was doing something inappropriate.

Paragraph 3

I have no doubt that we will one day abolish the death penalty in America. It will come sooner if people like me who know the truth about executions do our work well and educate the public. It will come slowly if we do not. Because, finally, I know that it is not a question of malice or ill will or meanness of spirit that prompts our citizens to support executions. It is, quite simply, that people don't know the truth of what is going on. That is not by accident. The secrecy surrounding executions makes it possible for executions to continue. I am convinced that if executions were made public, the torture and violence would be unmasked, and we would be shamed into abolishing executions. We would be embarrassed at the brutalization of the crowds that would gather to watch a man or woman being killed. And we would be humiliated to know that visitors from other countries — Japan, Russia, Latin America, Europe — were watching us kill our own citizens — we, who take pride in being the flagship of democracy in the world.

Paragraph 4

In the storied old days a person invented something in the attic or basement, got a patent on it, began building and selling it, and made a pile of money, all pretty much alone. Today's inventor, with some isolated exceptions, is likely to be a salaried lab hand working in almost complete anonymity for a large corporation. If he or she gets any reward for building a better mousetrap, it may only be a smile and a pat on the back from the supervisor. Those few individual inventors who do make it big — like Land, or Steve Wozniak of Apple Computer, or William Hewlett and David Packard of the company that bears their name — are all the more exceptional for being successful entrepreneurs and industrialists as well as inventors.

Paragraph 5

Holidays were once typically days of actual common celebration, of parades, ceremonies, feasts, songs, speeches, and marches. Today, most of this has been replaced by the public holiday's private competitor, the vacation.... The vacation is a relatively recent innovation, the product of bourgeois prosperity. The idea that wage earners could take paid vacations is an even more recent development, it only became widespread after World War I. It's fair to say that even in the 1930s and 1940s ordinary workers spent much more of their leisure time attending parades, carnivals, funerals, executions, and other communal events than they do today, and a good deal less time checking into motels. Today even solemn public holidays — holidays with as much contemporary meaning as Martin Luther King's birthday — are widely seen as simply more private leisure time, which is why we routinely fiddle with their dates to create three-day weekends.

Paragraph 6

There are many new terms and usages that seemed picky or unnecessary to conservatives when they appeared, but now are indispensable. What letterwriter, grateful for the coinage "Ms." Which lets one formally address women without referring to their marital status, would willingly go back to choosing between "Mrs." And "Miss"? There is a case to be made for "African-American", though it seems to have no marked advantages over "black" beyond its length, a quality of language many Americans mistake for dignity. Probably the term "Asian-American", vague as it is, is better than "Oriental", because it is at least decently neutral without the cloud of disparaging imagery that still clings to the older word. "Oriental" suggests a foreignness so extreme that it cannot be assimilated, and raises the Fu-Manchu phantoms of 19th-century racist fiction — treacherous cunning, clouds of opium, glittering slit eyes. "Native American" for American Indian, or just plain Indian, sounds virtuous, except that it carries with it the absurd implication that whites whose forebears may have been here for three, five, or even the whole thirteen generations that have elapsed since 1776 are in some way still interlopers, not "native" to this country. By the time whites get guilty enough to call themselves "European-Americans" it will be time to junk the whole lingo of nervous divisionism; everyone, black, yellow, red and white, can revert to being plain "Americans" again, as well they might.

Exercise 2

Sum up in two sentences the main idea of the following paragraph.

Knowing how to argue is a useful skill. We use it on ourselves in order to arrive at decisions; we use it with others as we discuss business strategies or policy changes on committees, as members of the local PTA, a law office, an environmental action group; we use it as fundraisers for a cause, like saving whales, we use it in applying for foundation grants and in drafting a letter to the editor of our hometown paper; we use it when we discuss child abuse, toxic waste, tax cuts, pothole repair, working mothers, and university investment policies. Our ability to express opinions persuasively — to present our views systematically as arguments — will allow us to make some difference in public life. If we lack the necessary skills, we are condemned to sit on the sidelines. Instead of doing the moving, we will be among the moved; more persuasive voices will convince us of what me must do. (pp. 222-223)

Exercise 3

Sum up in one sentence the writer's advice to people who want to stop violence, according to the passage.

Violence

Now, if you want to stop violence, if you want to stop wars, how much vitality, how much of yourself, do you give to it? Isn't it important to you that your children are killed, that your sons go into the army where they are bullied and butchered? Don't you care? My God, if that doesn't interest you, what does? Guarding your money? Having a good time? Taking drugs? Don't you see that this violence in yourself is destroying your children? Or do you see it only as some abstraction?

All right then, if you are interested, attend with all your heart and mind to find out. Don't just sit back and say, "Well, tell us all about it". I point out to you that you cannot look at anger nor at violence with eyes that condemn or justify and that if this violence is not a burning problem to you, you cannot put those two things away. So first you have to learn; you have to learn how to look at anger, how to look at your husband, your wife, your children; you have to listen to the politician, you have to learn why you are not objective, why you condemn or justify. You have to learn that you condemn and justify because it is part of the social structure you live in, your conditioning as a German or an Indian or a Negro or an American or whatever you happen to have been born, with all the dulling of the mind that this conditioning results in. To learn, to discover, something fundamental you must have the capacity to go deeply. If you have a blunt instrument, a dull instrument, you cannot go deeply. So what we are doing is sharpening the instrument which is the mind — the mind which has been made dull by all this justifying and condemning. You can penetrate deeply only if your mind is as sharp as a needle and as strong as a diamond.

It is no good just sitting back and asking, "How am I to get such a mind"? You have to want it as you want your next meal, and to have it you must see that what makes your mind dull and stupid is this sense of invulnerability which has built walls round itself and which is part of this condemnation and justification. If the mind can be rid of that, then you can look, study, penetrate, and perhaps come to a state that is totally aware of the whole problem.

To investigate the fact of your own anger you must pass non-judgemental on it, for the moment you conceive of its opposite you condemn it and therefore you cannot see it as it is. When you say you dislike or hate someone that is a fact, although it sounds terrible. If you look at it, go into it completely, it ceases, but if you say, "I must not hate; I must have love in my heart", then you are living in a hypocritical world with double standards. To live completely, fully, in the moment is to live with what is, the actual, without any sense of condemnation or justification — then you understand it so totally that you are finished with it. When you see clearly the problem is solved.

But can you see the face of violence clearly — the face of violence not only outside you but inside you, which means that you are totally free from violence because you have not admitted ideology through which to get rid of it? This requires very deep meditation, not just a verbal agreement or disagreement.

You have now read a series of statements but have you really understood? Your conditioned mind, your way of life, the whole structure of the society in which you live, prevent you from looking at a fact and being entirely free from it immediately. You say, "I will think about it; I will consider whether it is possible to be free from violence or not. I will try to be free." That is one of the most dreadful statements you can make, "I will try". There is no trying, no doing your best. Either you do it or you don't do it. You are admitting time while the house is burning. The house is burning as a result of the violence throughout the world and in yourself and you say, "Let me think about it. Which ideology is best to put out the fire?" When the house is on fire, do you argue about the colour of the hair of the man who brings the water?

Exercise 4

Write a one- sentence summary of the following passage.

... [Cleanthes, addressing himself to Demea]... Look round the world: Contemplate the whole and every part of it: You will find it to be nothing but one great machine, subdivided into an infinite number of lesser machines, which again admit of subdivisions, to a degree beyond what human senses and faculties can trace and explain. All these various machines, and even their most minute parts, are adjusted to each other with accuracy, which ravishes into admiration all men, who have ever contemplated them. The curious adapting of means to ends, throughout all nature, resembles exactly, though it much exceeds, the productions of human contrivance; of human design, thought, wisdom, and intelligence. Since therefore the effects resemble each other, we are led to infer, by all the rules of analogy, that the causes also resemble; and that the author of nature is somewhat similar to the mind of man; though possessed of much larger faculties, proportioned to the grandeur of the work, which he has executed. By this argument a posteriori, and by this argument alone, do we prove at once the existence of a deity, and his similarity to human mind and intelligence. (p. 53)

Exercise 5

Sum up in one paragraph the writer's ideas about drunk drivers, according to the passage.

No Compassion for Drunk Drivers

Roger Simon from the *Los Angeles Times*

I would like to make an admission up front: I have a thing about drunken drivers. I hate them. I really hate them.

Every time I read about another innocent person slaughtered by a drunken driver I become enraged.

So when I saw the nationally broadcast PBS special on drunken driving last week, I did not react as many did. I did not think it was sensitive and forthright.

I did not react as Phil Donahue, the host, did when he came on at the end and said: "I was enormously moved by this documentary, as I'm sure you were."

Not me, Phil. I wanted to kick the set in.

I was plenty moved for the victims. I was plenty moved for the people who were crippled, paralyzed, reduced to vegetables or dying. But the drunken drivers themselves did not hardly move me. I thought most got off easy.

First, let me tell you about the magnitude of the problem. Someone is killed by a drunk driver every 20 minutes in this country. On any given weekend night, on any road in America, 1 out of every 10 drivers is drunk.

And that is why drunken drivers will continue to get off easy, because so many of the lawmakers, so many of the jurors, so many of the judges have driven drunk themselves. They have a certain amount of sympathy for those who get caught.

The purpose of the documentary, called "Drinking and Driving: The Toll, The Tears," was to show that a drunken driver doesn't get off easy. Sometimes they go to jail, and sometimes they lose their licenses, and sometimes they lose their jobs, we are told.

But, in reality, they rarely do. Most drunken drivers get away with it. If they are caught, and few are, most go out and hire the best lawyers they can afford in order to beat the rap.

The elements that made this documentary special is that it was produced and written by Kelly Burke, 39, a Washington, D. C. television reporter. At 6:17 A. M. on July 1, 1984, after having 6 to 11 glasses of wine, his van crossed the center line and crashed head-on into a pick-up truck driven by Dennis Crouch, who was on his way to Army Reserve training.

Crouch was killed, leaving behind a son and a wife whom the report said 8 months pregnant.

After the accident, Burke's lawyer told reporters: "It's our feeling that there's a defense no matter what charges come down."

That line wasn't in the documentary, of course.

Burke's lawyer did a heck of a fine job, by the way. He was worth whatever he cost, because Burke's case was plea-bargained. In return for a guilty plea, the charge of homicide with a motor vehicle while intoxicated was dropped. Instead, Burke pleaded guilty to charges of driving under the influence and failing to stay in the proper lane.

His driver's license was revoked. He was sentenced to two years of unsupervised probation, fined $500, and ordered to produce a documentary on the results of drinking and driving.

But having seen Burke's documentary, I get the impression that one of the big results of his drinking and driving was getting exposure on national TV.

The show, which he also narrates, uses a lot of euphemisms.

Drivers are "impaired" after "imbibing". In one case, we are told that a drunk driver who killed a family of five "didn't mean it; he didn't even remember its happening."

But didn't he mean it? Don't all drunken drivers mean it? If you drink 6 to 11 glasses of wine, as Burke did, and then get behind the wheel, just what is it you do mean?

In the last segment, Burke comes on the screen. He stands there in a nice suit, and there is dramatic background music. He tells us about a driver, who pleaded guilty to driving under the influence of alcohol. This driver had worked "long hours and began celebrating." And then this driver crashed into a guy and he now suffers from a "melancholy paradoxically like that of the victims."

And, Burke tells us, this driver now is "bumming rides" and taking "buses and the subway" because his license was revoked. Legal fees are high. If this wasn't enough, "social activists kept saying he hadn't suffered enough."

Then Burke tells us: "I was the driver." Wrong, Mr. Burke.

You were the killer. So why don't you just say it?

A guy is dead, a woman widowed, two children orphaned, and Kelly Burke is telling me what agony it is to take public transportation.

As I said, I wanted to kick in the set. I admit my reaction to drunk driving is extreme. But Burke and I do agree on one thing: "I've said many times," he told the judge at the sentencing, "I wished it had been me."

If these self-indulgent slobs would just maim and kill each other, drunken driving wouldn't upset me as much.

In fact, it wouldn't upset me at all.

Unit 13 How to paraphrase?

13.1 What is paraphrase?

A paraphrase is a restatement of a text or passage in another form or other words, often to clarify meaning. It is your own interpretation of essential information and ideas expressed by someone else, presented in a new form. It is one legitimate way to borrow from a source. It is a more detailed restatement than a summary, which focuses concisely on a single main idea.

Unlike a summary that contains only the main idea(s) and supporting primary detail of a passage, a paraphrase literally recomposes every idea of someone else's composition into your own voice. It begins at the opening of a passage and then proceeds idea by idea to the end of the passage, leaving out none of the concepts.

13.2 Why to paraphrase?

Paraphrasing is a valuable skill because of the following three reasons. First, it is better than quoting information from an undistinguished passage. Second, it helps you control the temptation to quote too much. And third, the mental process required for successful paraphrasing helps you to grasp the full meaning of the original.

13.3 Length of paraphrases

Because the paraphrase includes every idea in a passage, it is often close to the same length as the original passage. However, if you explain the author's original statements in shorter phrases, the paraphrase can end up shorter than the passage.

13.4 How to paraphrase a source

There are some general advice to follow when you paraphrase a source.

(1) When reading a passage, try first to understand it as a whole, rather than pausing to write down specific ideas or phrases.

(2) Be selective. Most of the time you don't need to paraphrase an entire passage; instead, choose and summarize the material that helps you make a point in your paper.

(3) Remember that you can use direct quotations of phrases from the original within your paraphrase, and that you don't need to change or put quotation marks around shared language.

(4) Do not include your own ideas or commentary in the body of the summary or paraphrase. Your own ideas should come after the summary or paraphrase. You don't want your reader to become confused about which information is yours and which is the source's. And you always have to document summaries and paraphrases since the ideas are not your own.

Methods of Paraphrasing

While looking at the source, first change the structure, then the words. For example, consider the following passage from Love and Toil, in which the author, Ellen Ross, puts forth one of her major arguments.

Love and Toil maintains that family survival was the mother's main charge among the large majority of London's population who were poor or working class; the emotional and intellectual nurture of her child or children and even their actual comfort were forced into the background. To mother was to work for and organize household subsistence. (p.9)

Change the structure

At this stage, you might break up long sentences, combine short ones, expand phrases for clarity, or shorten them for conciseness.

Here's one of the many ways you might get started with a paraphrase of the passage above by changing its structure.

Children of the poor at the turn of the century received little if any emotional or intellectual nurturing from their mothers, whose main charge was family survival. Working for and organizing household subsistence were what defined mothering. Next to this, even the children's basic comfort was forced into the background (Ross, 1995).

Now you've succeeded in changing the structure, but the passage still contains many direct quotations, so you need to go on to the second step.

Change the words

Use synonyms or a phrase that expresses the same meaning. Leave shared language unchanged. The final paraphrase might look like this.

According to Ross (1993), poor children at the turn of the century received little mothering in our sense of the term. Mothering was defined by economic status, and among the poor, a mother's foremost responsibility was not to stimulate her children's minds or foster their emotional growth but to provide food and shelter to meet the basic requirements for physical survival. Given the magnitude of this task, children were deprived of even the "actual comfort" (p. 9) we expect mothers to provide today.

13.5 Paraphrase or quote ?

In general, use direct quotations only if you have a good reason. Most of your paper should be in your own words. Also, it's often conventional to quote more extensively from sources when you're writing a humanities paper, and to summarize from sources when you're writing in the social or natural sciences — but there are always exceptions.

In a **literary analysis paper**, for example, you'll want to quote from the literary text rather than summarize, because part of your task in this kind of paper is to analyze the specific words and phrases an author uses.

In **research papers**, you should **quote** from a source

- to show that an authority supports your point,
- to present a position or argument to critique or comment on,
- to include especially moving or historically significant language, and
- to present a particularly well-stated passage whose meaning would be lost or changed if paraphrased or summarized.

You should **summarize or paraphrase** when

- what you want from the source is the **idea** expressed, and **not the specific language** used to express it.

13.6 Examples

The original passage

Critical care nurses function in a hierarchy of roles. In this open heart surgery unit, the nurse manager hires and fires the nursing personnel. The nurse manager does not directly care for patients but follows the progress of unusual or long-term patients. On each shift a nurse assumes the role of resource nurse. This person oversees the hour-by-hour functioning of the unit as a whole, such as considering expected admissions and discharges of patients, ascertaining that beds are available for patients in the operating room, and covering sick calls. Resource nurses also take a patient assignment. They are the most experienced of all the staff nurses. The nurse clinician has a separate job description and provides for quality of care by orienting new staff, developing unit policies, and providing direct support where needed, such as assisting in emergency situations. The clinical nurse specialist in this unit is mostly involved with formal teaching in orienting new staff. The nurse manager, nurse clinician, and clinical nurse specialist are the designated experts. They do not take patient assignments. The resource nurse is seen as both a caregiver and a resource to other caregivers... Staff nurses have a hierarchy of seniority... Staff nurses are assigned to patients to provide all their nursing care. (Chase, 1995, p. 156)

The paraphrase

In her study of the roles of nurses in a critical care unit, Chase (1995) also found a hierarchy that distinguished the roles of experts and others. Just as the educational experts described above do not directly teach students, the experts in this unit do not directly attend to patients. That is the role of the staff nurses, who, like teachers, have their own "hierarchy of seniority" (p. 156). The roles of the experts include employing unit nurses and overseeing the care of special patients (nurse manager), teaching and otherwise integrating new personnel into the unit (clinical nurse specialist and nurse clinician), and policy-making (nurse clinician). In an intermediate position in the hierarchy is the resource nurse, a staff nurse with more experience than the others, who assumes direct care of patients as the other staff nurses do, but also takes on tasks to ensure the smooth operation of the entire facility.

Exercise 1

Write a paraphrase of each of the following sentences.
1. He had a good command of English.
2. He is not content with his present salary.
3. She has an appreciation of modern art.
4. Prevention is better than cure.
5. The teacher said, "Don't be late again, Bob."
6. Although it rained heavily they went swimming.
7. I had much difficulty in reading this book.
8. Nobody went short of coal that winter.
9. Tom goes in for sports.
10. I cannot put up with his laziness any longer.
11. Work hard and you will make progress.
12. We wouldn't have succeeded without their help.
13. You have a number of books from which you can choose.
14. We all expected you for the party last night.
15. As he waited for her he became impatient.
16. I was thinking of making a fresh start the next term and working hard.

Exercise 2

Write a paraphrase of each of the following sentences.
1. The little girl sat on the floor surrounded by a toy telephone, a rattle, a big plastic ball and a large number of highly colored building bricks.
2. The book contained information about such subjects as how a radio works, the development of radar and the splitting of the atom.
3. In the evenings he developed and printed his own films or amused himself with his stamp-collection or the radio he was making.
4. A railway train cannot run until the track has been laid. Ships need ports and quays. Lorries and cars need roadways. Aero planes need aerodromes with concrete runways. But a helicopter is free to go almost anywhere without anything built on the ground.
5. The man had plenty of things to occupy him that morning. He had overslept. The hotel had forgotten to call him and now he was late for an important business appointment. He dressed quickly, shaved hurriedly, grabbed his briefcase and hurried off down the hotel corridor.

Exercise 3

Rewrite each of the sentences, using the words in parentheses.
1. People trying to interpret a situation often look at those around them to see how to react. (base reactions on)

2. There are three things bystanders must do if they are to intervene in an emergency. (necessary)
3. In a crowd, then, each person is less likely to notice a potential emergency than when alone. (tends to...less)
4. Even if a person defines an event as an emergency... (decides)
5. ... the presence of other bystanders may still make each person less likely to intervene. (may feel less inclined)

Exercise 4

Write a summary and a paraphrase of the following passage.

　　Students frequently overuse direct quotation in taking notes, and as a result they overuse quotations in the final [research] paper. Probably only about 10% of your final manuscript should appear as directly quoted matter. Therefore, you should strive to limit the amount of exact transcribing of source materials while taking notes. Lester, James D. *Writing Research Papers*. 2nd ed. (1976): 46-47.

Exercise 5

Write a paraphrase of each of the following passages.

1. "The Antarctic is the vast source of cold on our planet, just as the sun is the source of our heat, and it exerts tremendous control on our climate," [Jacques] Cousteau told the camera. "The cold ocean water around Antarctica flows north to mix with warmer water from the tropics, and its upwelling help to cool both the surface water and our atmosphere. Yet the fragility of this regulating system is now threatened by human activity." From Captain Cousteau, Audubon (May 1990):17.
2. The twenties were the years when drinking was against the law, and the law was a bad joke because everyone knew of a local bar where liquor could be had. They were the years when organized crime ruled the cities, and the police seemed powerless to do anything against it. Classical music was forgotten while jazz spread throughout the land, and men like Bix Beiderbecke, Louis Armstrong, and Count Basie became the heroes of the young. The flapper was born in the twenties, and with her bobbed hair and short skirts, she symbolized, perhaps more than anyone or anything else, America's break with the past. From Kathleen Yancey, English 102 Supplemental Guide (1989): 25.
3. Of the more than 1 000 bicycling deaths each year, three-fourths are caused by head injuries. Half of those killed are school-age children. One study concluded that wearing a bike helmet can reduce the risk of head injury by 85 percent. In an accident, a bike helmet absorbs the shock and cushions the head. From Bike Helmets: Unused Lifesavers, Consumer Reports (May 1990): 348.
4. Matisse is the best painter ever at putting the viewer at the scene. He's the most realistic of all modern artists, if you admit the feel of the breeze as necessary to a

landscape and the smell of oranges as essential to a still life. "The Casbah Gate" depicts the well-known gateway Bab el Aassa, which pierces the southern wall of the city near the sultan's palace. With scrubby coats of ivory, aqua, blue, and rose delicately fenced by the liveliest gray outline in art history, Matisse gets the essence of a Tangier afternoon, including the subtle presence of the bowaab, the sentry who sits and surveys those who pass through the gate. From Peter Plagens, Bright Lights. Newsweek (26 March 1990): 50.

5. While the Sears Tower is arguably the greatest achievement in skyscraper engineering so far, it's unlikely that architects and engineers have abandoned the quest for the world's tallest building. The question is: Just how high can a building go? Structural engineer William LeMessurier has designed a skyscraper nearly one-half mile high, twice as tall as the Sears Tower. And architect Robert Sobel claims that existing technology could produce a 500-story building. From Ron Bachman, Reaching for the Sky. Dial (May 1990): 15.

Unit 14　Expressing your voice in a research paper

14.1　What is voice?

In writing, voice is the way your writing "sounds" on the page. It has to do with the way you write, the tone you take — friendly, formal, chatty, distant — the words you choose — everyday words or formal words — the pattern of your sentences, and the way these things fit in — or not — with the personality of the writer and the style of your writing. A writer's voice is the impression or image of the writer projected in his writing. This image is composed of the various characteristics or attributes of personality that the words and sentences convey. Sometimes, this image is called the author's *persona*.

14.2　The features of voice in academic writing

The first defining characteristic of voice found in academic or scholarly writing is the language of scholarship. The *language of scholarship* uses the expressions of what is called "Standard English." Those are the words and phrases and even sentence patterns most frequently used by the general public to convey information in written communication. It refrains from the use of various informal patterns and expressions found in colloquial or spoken English as well as slang. It is less formal than those expressions found in ceremonial language. At the same time, scholarly language employs the jargon appropriate to the various academic disciplines. The field of psychology, for example, has its unique expressions just as does biology and the other sciences, or the study of literature, marketing, or history.

The tone of academic writing is one of openness and objectivity. You should try to convey in your writing an openmindedness to ideas, even when ideas of others may conflict or contrast dramatically with your own. You want to convey a sense of objectivity. You do this by avoiding intensely emotional language, seemingly biased or slanted references.

14.3　Factors that influence the effective use of voice

1) *Use of first person*

Appropriately or inappropriately, your use of first person makes voice dominant as a persuasive element. Generally, avoid using the first person pronouns of "I" and "we" in academic writing; unless you are the respected authority in the field, first person may be interpreted as arrogant.

2) *Well-organized writing*

A paper that seems to build upon a plan or outline, a discussion that seems to progress in a controlled direction invites the confidence of your readers. At the same time, an unorganized paper makes you look scattered and distracted. You are likely to earn little respect and appreciation for your efforts and ideas.

3) *Edited writing*

A paper free from mechanical, stylistic, and grammatical problems maintains the confidence a reader. Most important, it communicates clearly. Justifiably, readers will feel patronized by being asked to read careless work.

4) *Objective diction*

Use words which convey openness. Avoid slanted words which might reflect a bias on your subject. Avoid hostile and provocative words.

5) *Appropriate diction*

Use words that complement the level of expertise of your audience. Don't be condescending to your readers. Don't patronize them with words that are going to make you appear haughty or arrogant.

6) *Level of development*

Don't overwork *secondary development* (explanation of explanation) in your paragraphs.

7) *Emotional language*

Try to effect a balance between your use of conceptual words and emotionally-impacted words. Papers which promote unnatural emotion may turn readers off to your message.

14.4 Appropriate use of voice in academic writing

The voice you convey in a composition can be a powerful persuasive element in academic writing. A strong voice reflecting the positive attributes discussed above will complement and help you achieve your purpose as a writer. Used inappropriately, however, it can undermine even the most carefully reasoned argument.

The use of voice can be classified according to three traditional roles: *the reporter, the interpreter, and the critic.*

1) *The reporter*

The "reporter" conveys information, presents the "facts" of a subject to the reading audience through summaries, paraphrases, allusions to, or quotations of sources, and through analysis, definition, and illustration of primary sources.

2) *The interpreter*

If the "reporter" presents the facts, the "interpreter" explains their meaning(s).

3) *The critic*

The "critic" evaluates the facts explained by the "interpreter." As a judge, the "critic" can render either a favorable or unfavorable verdict. Argumentation is the framework of judgmental conclusions.

These three roles are, of course, the primary functions of what more generally is referred to as analysis (though specifically, the function of the "reporter" is analysis).

14.5　Editing and revising for voice

Be alert to the image of yourself you are projecting in your writing. You can always make changes in your drafts which will either mute your voice or make it more prominent, depending on the importance, of course, of such "presence" in your composition.

Exercise 1

Comment on the voice in the following text. You may organize your ideas from the following aspects.

1. The writer's care about the topic.
2. The writer's strong feelings.
3. The writer's individuality.
4. The authenticity of the writing.
5. The originality of the writing.
6. The writer's personality.
7. The purpose of the writing.
8. The tone of the writing.
9. The intended audience of the writing.

Chores!

Chores! Chores! Chores! Chores are boring! Scrubbing toilets, cleaning sinks, and washing bathtubs take up a lot of my time and are not fun at all.

Toilets! When you're scrubbing toilets make sure they are not stinky. I've scrubbed one before and I was lucky it didn't stink. I think toilets are one of the hardest things to scrub in the bathroom because it is hard to get up around the rim.

Sinks are one of the easiest things to clean in the bathroom because they have no rims and they are small. I have cleaned one before and it was pretty easy.

Bathtubs, ever washed one? They are big, they are deep, and it is hard to get up around the sides. The bathtub is the hardest, I think, to wash in the bathroom.

All chores are boring, especially making my bed. Cleaning my room is OK because I have to organize, and I like organizing. Dusting is the worst: dust, set down, pick up, dust, set down. There are so many things to dust, and it's no fun.

Chores aren't the worst but they're definitely not the best!

Exercise 2

What is the tone of the writer in the following text? Why do you think the writer uses this tone in the text ?

How to argue effectively

I argue very well. Ask any of my remaining friends. I can win an argument on any topic, against any opponent. People know this and steer clear of me at parties. Often, as a sign of their great respect, they don't even invite me. You too can win arguments.

Simply follow these rules.

Drink liquor

Suppose you are at a party and some hotshot intellectual is expounding on the economy of Peru, a subject you know nothing about. If you're drinking some health-fanatic drink like grapefruit juice, you'll hang back, afraid to display your ignorance, while the hotshot enthralls your date. But if you drink several large martinis, you'll discover you have STRONG VIEWS about the Peruvian economy. You'll be a WEALTH of information. You'll argue forcefully, offering searing insights and possibly upsetting furniture. People will be impressed. Some may leave the room.

Make things up

Suppose, in the Peruvian economy argument, you are trying to prove that Peruvians are underpaid, a position you base solely on the fact that YOU are underpaid. DON'T say: "I think Peruvians are underpaid." Say instead: "The average Peruvian's salary in 1981 dollars adjusted for the revised tax base is $1 452.81 per annum, which is $836.07 before the mean gross poverty level."

NOTE: Always make up exact figures

If an opponent asks you where you got your information, make THAT up too. Say: "This information comes from Dr. Hovel T. Moon's study for the Buford Commission published on May 9, 1982. Didn't you read it?"

. . . .

Unit 15   How to synthesizing information

15.1   What is a synthesis?

Synthesis means putting ideas from many sources together in your writing. For example, after reading several books, watching movies and participating in a variety of activities, you may want to organize some of the information around a theme or a question, make generalizations, and then present information in a logical way to support your argument.

A synthesis is not a summary, a comparison or a review. Rather a synthesis is a result of an integration of what you heard/read and your ability to use this learning to develop and support a key thesis or argument in your research paper.

Your ability to write syntheses depends on your ability to infer relationships among sources — essays, articles, fiction, and also some other types of sources, such as lectures, interviews, observations. This ability is important in writing research papers, because in your writing, you have to make explicit the relationships that you have inferred among separate sources.

Before you're in a position to draw relationships between two or more sources, you must understand what those sources say; that is to say, you must be able to summarize these sources. It will frequently be helpful for your readers if you provide at least partial summaries of sources in your synthesis. At the same time, you must go beyond summary to make judgments — judgments based on your critical reading of your sources. You should already have drawn some conclusions about the quality and validity of these sources; and you should know how much you agree or disagree with the points made in your sources and the reasons for your agreement or disagreement.

Because a synthesis is based on two or more sources, you will need to be selective when choosing information from each. It would be neither possible nor desirable, for instance, to discuss every point that the authors of two books make about their subject. What you must do is select the ideas and information from each source that best allow you to achieve your purpose.

15.2   Synthesis and your writing purpose

Your purpose in reading source materials and then in drawing upon them to write your own material is often determined by the purpose of your research paper. Your purpose determines not only what parts of your sources you will use but also how you will relate them to one another. Since the very essence of synthesis is the combining of information and ideas, you must have some basis on which to combine them. Some relationships among the material in you sources must make them worth synthesizing. Therefore, the better able you are to discover such relationships, the better able you will be to use your sources in writing syntheses. Your purpose in writing will determine how you relate your source materials to one another. Your purpose in writing determines which sources you use, which parts of them you use, at which points in your essay you use them, and in what manner you relate them to one another.

15.3 Two types of syntheses

Generally speaking, there are two types of syntheses: the explanatory synthesis and the argument synthesis. An explanatory synthesis helps readers to understand a topic. Writers explain when they divide a subject into its component parts and present them to the reader in a clear and orderly fashion. Explanations may entail descriptions that re-create in words some object, place, event, sequence of events, or state of affairs. The purpose in writing an explanatory essay is not to argue a particular point, but rather to present the facts in a reasonably objective manner. Although a research paper is basically argumentative, at times it will include sections that are explanatory in nature.

The purpose of an argument synthesis is for you to present your own point of view — supported, of course, by relevant facts, drawn from sources, and presented in a logical manner. The thesis of an argumentative essay is debatable. It makes a proposition about which reasonable people could disagree, and any two writers working with the same source materials could conceive of and support other, opposite theses.

15.4 Using synthesis in your writing

Synthesis is the opposite of analysis. Analysis is the process of breaking something down — a situation, a problem, an argument, a decision — and examining the elements of it. In synthesis you bring together parts and make a whole that is logical and coherent.

In writing, this means incorporating facts and opinions from other writers, along with your own thesis and ideas, into a smoothly flowing text. This is one of the most common tasks facing writers in many academic disciplines and professions. The use of sources is important in academic and professional life as few of us are experts, and even experts must provide evidence to support a claim.

Synthesis writing depends on sources written by others; in order to use those sources correctly, the writer needs to have good summarizing and paraphrasing skills as well as the ability to analyze. You can comment on others' ideas more efficiently if you can compress what you've read into a summary. And your writing about others' ideas will be stronger if you don't assume all published information is valid — if you can analyze and evaluate what you read.

The following are some guidelines for using sources with the goal of writing a synthesis of your own ideas with support and evidence from those sources.

Before you write:
- Find and evaluate sources related to your topic.
- Use the sources to educate yourself. What are the facts? What are the controversies?

- Develop your own perspective about the topic. This will become your thesis.

When writing:
- Write your ideas and develop them logically.
- Use factual information from the sources as needed.
- Use paraphrased information from experts, or use brief quotations if the wording is particularly striking or powerful.
- Give proper citation.
- If appropriate, use an author's name, a reporting verb, and information about the source to establish credibility.
- Provide coherence between your ideas and those of your sources.

When you are synthesizing information in your research paper, you should also keep the following advice in your mind.

1. Have a well-formulated thesis written out before you begin writing your essay or article. Develop a limited number of supporting arguments and express them in complete sentences also. This can serve as an outline to follow and can help you stay on track as you develop your ideas in writing.
2. Begin each paragraph with a topic sentence that directly relates to your thesis. The complete sentences you write in your outline (see above) can serve this function. After your point is clearly stated in one or more sentences, material from your sources can be brought in as evidence.
3. Provide proper citation when using the words or ideas of others. If you name a source in the text, tell enough about the person or source to establish credibility.
4. Select information carefully and present it to the reader skillfully. The emphasis is on what you have to say, not what the sources have to say, so the "voice," or tone, is yours. For this reason, a writer using sources usually paraphrases information rather than quoting and provides enough explanation to incorporate the paraphrased information logically and coherently.
5. It is not necessary to provide ALL the evidence you find in your sources. Select the most powerful evidence and decide how to present it most effectively — through paraphrasing, quoting, or a graphic representation such as a chart or a graph.

15.5 Examples of using synthesis in your writing

Now we will look at some examples of using synthesis in writing research papers. In the following example of a synthesis paragraph, a student writer has integrated the ideas of the two sources together and indicated how the views of the sources relate to one another.

> On the issue of teaching methods for recent immigrants, Santiago believes that total immersion is useless, since students cannot learn in a language they do not understand. He claims that students find it overwhelming to learn a new language all at once and that they, therefore, learn best in bilingual classroom. Hayakawa, however,

> believes that immersion into a language to be the fastest way to learn that language and thereby gain entry into the majority culture. These disagreements, perhaps, can be explained in term of contrasting philosophical views of American culture. Santiago operates with the "salad bowl" metaphor, the belief that America is a rich nation precisely because of its distinctive ethnic groups. Hayakawa operates with a "melting pot" metaphor, the belief that in coming to America foreigners should relinquish what makes them separate (i. e. their language) in order to blend into the American mainstream.

However, the above paragraph does not quite meet the requirements of writing the research paper, because the writer fails to give enough information about the sources he quotes from.

In the next paragraph, the writer cites the sources properly. We can infer from the passage that he has consulted four sources: Source A (Bound 2002); Source B (Robertson 2003); Source C (Havir 1999) and Source D (Kerstjens 2000). We can also find out that the ideas of Bond and Robertson are in contradiction with those of Havir and Kerstjens.

> Supporting the contention that English is the dominant world language, Bond (2002) and Robertson (2003) points out its importance as the medium of international communication in business, technology and other global forums. However, others argue that despite its apparent dominance, English is not the global language when the number of native speakers of other languages, e. g. Chinese, are considered. (Havir 1999; Kerstjens 2000)

Exercise 1

Read the articles below and, in a paragraph of not more than 250 words, discuss the problems for the human race with regard to water. Cite any sources you use.

> **Water H_2O**
>
> The commonest molecular compound on Earth; a liquid, freezing to ice at 0 ℃ and boiling to steam at 100 ℃. It covers about 75% of the Earth's surface, and dissolves almost everything to some extent. It is essential to life, and occurs in all living organisms. It is strongly hydrogen-bonded in the liquid phase, and co-ordinates to dissolved ions. Unusually, the solid is less dense than the liquid; this results in ice floating on ponds, and accounts for the destructiveness of continued freezing and thawing. Water containing substantial concentrations of calcium and magnesium ions is called "hard", and is "softened" by replacing these ions with sodium or potassium, which do not form insoluble products with soaps.
> From: *The Cambridge Encyclopaedia* by David Crystal. It was published in Cambridge by Cambridge University Press in 1990 and the extract is from page 1285.)

Crisis and challenge

Today in almost every area of the world one chooses to look at there is a water problem — scarcity, depletion, pollution, lack of sanitation, failing rains due to global warming, big dam projects blocking up rivers, privatisation, inequities of distribution, cross-border conflict, profligate use and mismanagement. Take your pick. But let's start with overuse.

We learn at school that freshwater on earth follows a cycle: it is constantly being replenished, some of it soaking into the ground and into vegetation, some of it meandering through streams and rivers on its way back to the sea. But at what stage of our lives do we forget this important lesson? The moment one starts using freshwater beyond the rate at which it can be replenished, the hydrological cycle is endangered.

The crisis is particularly acute in relation to our groundwater reserves, lying deep under the surface in aquifers, upon which a third of the world's population depends. Water can take thousands of years to percolate into aquifers (some contain water from the last ice age). Some have since sealed up, allowing little possibility of recharge. Because the reserves of water they hold are large, humans have been tapping them like there is no tomorrow. Currently we are pumping out about 200 billion cubic metres (1 cubic metre = 908 litres) more than can be recharged, steadily using up our water capital.

Take California with its manicured lawns and 560 000 swimming pools. Having taxed the Colorado River to the limit, the region's aquifers are being guzzled up. By 2020 officials predict a water shortfall nearly equivalent to what the state is currently using. Another more distant water source needs to be found to gulp down. Consumption is the operative word for US water use.

(From an article by Dinar Godrej called "Precious fluid". It was published the *New Internationalist* magazine, volume 354. It was published in, March 2003 on pages 9-12. This extract is from page 10.)

The ocean

Approximately three fourths of this earth of ours is covered by the ocean, which modifies its climate, receives its sediments, and determines the configuration of its shores. It has been estimated that the average depth of the ocean is about 2.25 miles and the average height of the continents about 0.5 mile, so that if all of the land were cut off at sea level and placed in the ocean basins, it would fill only one fortieth of the depression. The term average depth does not give a true picture of the ocean floor, which contains islands that rise 3 or 4 miles above a general level and depressions or deeps that descend about an equal distance. Off the coast of the Philippine Islands is the greatest known depression 35 433 feet deep and the Tuscarora Deep near Japan exceeds 28 000 feet. In the Atlantic soundings over 27 000 feet have been recorded near

Puerto Rico. The great deeps of the ocean are of approximately the same magnitude as the highest elevations on land, for Mt. Everest, the highest measured mountain, exceeds 29 000 feet.

(By Doctor Victor T. Allen, MS, PhD. This is from an old book called *This earth of ours*. It was published in 1939 in Milwaukee by The Bruce Publishing Company. This section is from page 160.)

- On our blue planet 97.5% of the water is saltwater, unfit for human use.
- The majority of freshwater is beyond our reach, locked into polar snow and ice.
- Less than 1% of freshwater is usable, amounting to only 0.01% of the Earth's total water.
- Even this would be enough to support the world's population three times over if used with care.
- However, water — like population — isn't distributed evenly. Asia has the greatest annual availability of fresh-water and Australia the lowest. But when population is taken into account the picture looks very different.
- Our increasing thirst is a result of growing population, industrial development and the expansion of irrigated farming. In the past 40 years, the area of irrigated land has doubled.
- By the mid-1990s, 80 countries home to 40% of world population encountered serious water shortages. Worst affected are Africa and the Middle East.
- By 2025 two-thirds of the world's people will be facing water stress. The global demand for water will have grown by — over 40% by then.
- The only ray of hope is that the growth in actual use of water has been slower than predicted.
- Dirty water is the cause of numerous diseases, but improving hygiene and sanitation are equally important in order to curb water-related diseases.

(From an article in *New Internationalist* called Water: The facts. It was on page 18 of the March 2003 issue. This was volume 354.)

Water pollution

Water pollution affects oceans, streams, rivers, lakes, ponds, and groundwater, and can be caused by natural impurities or human activities that pollute the nearby water or water supplies.

Natural impurities in water are sometimes, but not always, pollutants. They are divided into three categories of particles: suspended particles that absorb light and make water cloudy, such as beach sand, coal dust, and bacteria; colloidal particles, such as soot and some viruses, which cannot be removed from water by ordinary filtration and cause the water to look cloudy when observed at right angles to a beam of light; and dissolved matter, which are the smallest impurities in water, including molecules and ions of various substances, such as chloride or sodium ions or carbon dioxide molecules.

Human activities are often the cause of localized water pollution, as water becomes contaminated with heavy metals, toxic chemicals, and bacteria. Rivers may experience oil and chemical spills, untreated sewage runoff from homes and industry, and nonpoint source pollution, such as contaminated runoff from highways, parking lots, and agricultural fields. Groundwater (or subsurface water) may be contaminated by the infiltration of pollutants from landfills and septic tanks, or by percolation of water containing contaminated runoff. Parts of the ocean are sometimes polluted by oil tanker spills and garbage dumping.

(This was written by Patricia Barnes-Svarney, in *The New York public library science desk reference*. It was published in New York by Macmillan in 1996 and this paragraph is from page 472.)

Some 1.2 billion people lack access to clean water, twice that number have no sanitation, and most of the world will not have enough water within 30 years. This combination of scarcity and bad management affects food supplies, health, education, nature and economic development. It means women spend long periods collecting it, families spend up to half their daily income on it, farmers lose their land, and infants die.

Global consumption of freshwater is doubling every 20 years and new sources are becoming scarcer and more expensive to develop and treat.

In 1996, says the UN, humanity used about 54% of all the accessible freshwater contained in rivers, lakes and underground aquifers. This is conservatively projected to climb to at least 70% by 2025, reflecting population growth alone, and by much more if per capita consumption rises at its current pace.

Some 70% of all the world's fresh water used by man goes to grow food, and in parts of the US, North Africa and Asia, farmers can take up to 95%. Unavoidable population increases in the next 20 years will mean that agriculture alone will need at least 17% more water than it does now just to grow the extra food these people will need.

(Blue gold: Earth's liquid asset John Vidal, *The Guardian*, August 2002, p. 6.)

Unit 16 Reporting verbs

16.1 Introduction

In academic writing it will often be necessary to refer to the research of others and to report on their findings. In order to do so, we have to use reporting verbs such as "Evans (1994) **suggests** that...", "Brown (2001) **argues** that..."

The difficulty with using reporting verbs is that there are many different verbs, and each of them has slightly different, and often subtle, meaning. Using the correct words relies on making the correct interpretation of what the writer you are studying is saying.

16.2 Different reporting verbs

Reporting verbs differ in terms of their strength — for example "to suggest" is much weaker, and more tentative, than "to argue". The two verbs convey very different pictures about how the author you are studying sees his or her materials and research.

Some reporting verbs are used principally to say what the writer does and does not do. These verbs do not indicate any value judgement on the part of the writer — they are called "neutral" reporting verbs.

A second group of verbs is used to show when the writer has an inclination to believe something but still wishes to be hesitant — we call these "tentative" reporting verbs.

Finally, if the writer has strong arguments to put forward and is absolutely sure of his or her ground, we can use "strong" reporting verbs to refer to these ideas.

Obviously, it is important to ensure that we **interpret** the writer's ideas correctly. For instance, if we say "Jones (1999) argues..." rather than "Jones (1999) suggests...", there is a major difference of meaning. The first indicates strength — the second tentativity. It is very important, in academic writing, not to misinterpret a writer's intentions when we are reporting them.

In the table below, the main reporting verbs in English are classified in terms of their function, and their strength.

Function and strength	Example verbs
NEUTRAL: verbs used to say what the writer describes in factual terms, demonstrates, refers to, and discusses, and verbs used to explain his/her methodology.	describe, show, reveal, study, demonstate, note, point out, indicate, report, observe, assume, take into consideration, examine, go on to say that, state, believe (unless this is a strong belief), mention, etc.

Function and strength	Example verbs
TENTATIVE: verbs used to say what the writer suggests or speculates on (without being absolutely certain).	suggest, speculate, intimate, hypothesise, moot, imply, propose, recommend, posit the view that, question the view that, postulate, etc.
STRONG: verbs used to say what the writer makes strong arguments and claims for.	argue, claim, emphasise, contend, maintain, assert, theorize, support the view that, deny, negate, refute, reject, challenge, strongly believe that, counter the view/argument that, etc.

16.3 Reporting verbs and your point of view

When discussing an author's work, reporting verbs can be used to great effect. For example, the reporting verb you select to introduce your discussion/comments can either indicate **your viewpoint** regarding the accuracy of the literature (i.e. correct, neither correct/incorrect, incorrect), or it can indicate the **author's viewpoint** regarding the content of the literature (i.e. positive or negative).

The following is a list of possible reporting verbs indicating, from **your viewpoint**:
- a belief that the literature is correct;
- a neutral attitude towards the veracity of the literature (i.e. neither correct nor incorrect);
- a belief that the literature is incorrect.

writer's attitude towards the literature being cited	CORRECT	NEUTRAL	INCORRECT	
Reporting verbs These are usually in 3rd person singular or plural simple present tense form. E.g. Brown (2004) explains ... Smith and Bull (2003) explain ...	acknowledges	adds	indicates	
	defines	argues	informs	
	demonstrates	claims	presents	
	explains	clarifies	proposes	confuses
	identifies	concludes	remarks	disregards
	observes	describes	reminds	ignores
	outlines	expresses	reports	
	shows	feels	states	
	throws light on	finds	uses	

Examples

1. Stein-Parbury (2000) **defines** listening **as** the ability to hear, understand, and appreciate a patient's experience.

2. De Cieri et al. (2003) **clarify** the role of human resources in terms of a company's improved competitiveness in their Australian Business Excellence Model.
3. In their presentation, Sawyer and Smith (2001) **described** their sampling methods and data analysis in great detail.
4. In their study on acculturation, Birman, Sharpe, and Angeles (2004) **propose** a variety of solutions to the current problem facing Australian cities such as Melbourne and Sydney, that of "ghettoisation" (p. 77).
5. Previous studies on the work-study balance of tertiary students (Campbell, 2004; Guthrie, Logan, & Tuomy, 2003; Smith, 1999) **concluded that** most students prioritise work over study.
6. Lygon (2001) **ignores** conflicting data in his review of the literature thereby compromising the credibility of his research in the field.

16.4　Reporting verbs and the author's point of view

It is also possible to indicate, by careful selection of the appropriate reporting verb, whether the author is positive or negative in their attitude to the content of the literature being cited.

What follows is a list of possible reporting verbs indicating, from the **author's viewpoint**:

- a positive attitude towards the content of the literature;
- a negative or uncertain attitude towards the content of the literature.

Author's attitude towards the content being discussed	POSITIVE			NEGATIVE/UNCERTAIN	
Reporting verbs These are usually in 3rd person singular or plural simple present tense form. E.g. Brown (2004) insists... Smith and Bull (2003) insist...	accepts	insists	remarks	attacks	opposes
	advises	maintains	stresses	challenges	questions
	affirms	notes	subscribes to	disagrees	rejects
	agrees	praises	suggests	dismisses	suspects
	applauds	points out	supports	disputes	warns
	asserts	posits	thinks	doubts	
	concurs	recommends	urges	mistrusts	

Examples

1. Taib (2003) and Partridge (2003) **concur that** the most effective way of improving second language proficiency is through social and linguistic immersion in a country's culture and society.
2. Bertrand and Sullivan (2002) **note that** in order to succeed academically, children require strict discipline at home as well as at school.
3. Along with others in their field, Noonan and Williams (2002) **subscribe to** the theory that carefully selected domestic animals have a positive role to play in the palliative care

of children and adults.

4. Beaumont (1998) **challenges** many long-held beliefs amongst the medical fraternity about mind-body-spirit connections.
5. In their thorough review of related literature, Scederis et al. (2000) **dismiss** previous studies' findings relating to the use of Royal Jelly to treat asthmatics.
6. Kennedy (1998) **questions** the claims made in Beaumont's paper (1998) on the role of meditation amongst sufferers of post-traumatic stress.

16.5 Usage patterns of reporting verbs

Reporting verbs can be used in your research paper to indicate your attitude to the sources you cite. But these verbs are used in different patterns. The following are some grammatical patterns to follow in using these verbs.

Pattern 1: *reporting verb* + *that* + *subject* + *verb*

acknowledge	admit	agree	allege	argue
assert	assume	believe	claim	conclude
consider	decide	demonstrate	deny	determine
discover	doubt	emphasize	explain	find
hypothesize	imply	indicate	infer	note
object	observe	point out	prove	reveal
say	show	state	suggest	think

Examples

(a) Da Souza **argues that** previous researchers have misinterpreted the data.

(b) Researchers **have demonstrated that** the procedure is harmful.

(c) Positivists **find that** social disorders are exacerbated by class factors.

(d) Singh **infers that** both states are essential.

Note that these verbs all differ in meaning — they cannot be used interchangeably. For example, the verb argue in sample sentence (a) indicates your judgement that the author's conclusion is based on evidence and reasoning, but that other conclusions might be possible. The verb demonstrate in sentence (b) indicates your judgement that the researchers' evidence and reasoning are so convincing that no other conclusion is possible.

Beware of using the verbs discuss or express followed by that. For example, it is incorrect to write, "The reviewer expressed that the movie is not worth seeing." You can, however, write the following: "The reviewer expressed the view that the movie is not worth seeing."

Verbs in this category may also appear in a subordinate clause beginning with as:

(a) As Da Souza argues, misinterpretations by previous researchers need to be corrected.

(b) As researchers have demonstrated, the procedure is harmful.

Pattern 2: *reporting verb* + *somebody/something* + **for** + *noun/gerund*

| applaud | blame | censure | criticize | disparage |
| fault | praise | ridicule | single out | thank |

Examples

(a) Smith **criticized** Jones **for** his use of incomplete data (OR **for** using incomplete data).

(b) Both Smith and Jones **condemn** previous researchers **for** distorting the data.

(c) Banting **thanked** Best **for** his contribution to the discovery of insulin.

Pattern 3: *reporting verb + somebody/something + as + noun/gerund/adjective*

appraise	assess	characterize	class	classify
define	depict	describe	evaluate	identify
interpret	portray	present	refer	view

Examples

(a) Jones **describes** the findings **as** resting on irrefutable evidence.

(b) Smith **identifies** the open window **as** a source of contamination.

(c) Smith and Jones both **present** their data **as** conclusive.

16.6 Language points to be considered when using reporting verbs

The structure of sentences when using reporting verbs can vary, and can be flexible.

e.g.

Jones (1999) argues, in his study of thermodynamics, that...

As Jones (1999) argues in his study of thermodynamics,...

In his study of thermodynamics, Jones (1999) argues that...

It is possible (and often quite attractive stylistically) to invert the subject and verb when reporting.

e.g. Thermodynamics, Jones (1999) argues, is...

Reporting the work of others often needs an extra sentence introduction or "lead-in".

e.g. In considering Smith's discussion on thermodynamics, Jones (1999) argues that...

Exercise 1

Match the reporting verbs below with their definitions.

1. admit	a) a remark that calls attention to something or someone
2. advise	b) state firmly
3. announce	c) announce publicly or officially
4. assure	d) make (someone) agree, understand, or realise the truth of something
5. claim	e) impart knowledge of some fact or event to someone
6. complain	f) give advice
7. confirm	g) refuse to give up or change your mind

8. convince	h) define and make understandable
9. declare	i) give or restore confidence
10. explain	j) make a proposal, declare a plan for something
11. inform	k) strengthen or make more firm
12. insist	l) an assertion that something is true or factual
13. mention	m) declare to be true
14. persuade	n) express discontent, displeasure, or unhappiness
15. reassure	o) inform with certainty and confidence
16. suggest	p) cause somebody to adopt a certain position, belief, or course of action

Exercise 2

Match the sentences with the reporting verbs.

1. I'll carry the suitcase.   A. advised
2. Would you like to have dinner?   B. offered
3. I won't wear my new dress!   C. refused
4. Please, please let me stay up!   D. reminded
5. You shouldn't smoke too much.   E. begged
6. Don't forget to post the letter.   F. invited

Exercise 3

Match the sentences with the reporting verbs.

1. Please, please, let me come with you! A. reminded
2. You should go home and go to bed.   B. ordered
3. Don't forget to lock the door.   C. begged
4. Switch that mobile phone off!   D. admitted
5. I did once steal some chewing gum.   E. complained
6. This soup tastes like hot water!   F. advised

Exercise 4

Change the direct speech to reported speech. Use short forms.

"I'll arrive at six." She said she _____ at six.

"You shouldn't smoke." He told me I _____.

"Why are you crying?" I asked him why he _____.

"Mel left today." He said Mel _____ that day.

"We are not married." She said they _____.

Exercise 5

Fill the gaps using the verbs in the box. Use each verb once only.

advise   hope   promise   suggest   beg   insist   remind   threaten   deny   invite refuse   warn

1. "I didn't do it," she said.
   She _____ doing it.
2. "Have lunch with me," she said.
   She _____ me to have lunch with her.
3. "Why don't you buy one?" said Tom.
   Tom _____ I buy one.
4. "I promise I'll take you to Prague," said Mary.
   Mary _____ to take me to Prague.
5. "I hope Andy phones tonight," said Clare.
   Clare _____ Andy would phone that night.
6. "Please, please don't tell anyone!" he said.
   He _____ me not to tell anyone.
7. "I won't do it," he said.
   He _____ to do it.
8. "You should have lessons," she said.
   She _____ me to have lessons.
9. "We really must go with you," they said.
   They _____ on going with me.
10. "Don't forget to phone Granny," said Mum.
    Mum _____ me to phone Granny.
11. "If you wear my T-shirt again, I'll pinch you very hard," said Maggy.
    Maggie _____ to pinch me very hard if I wore her T-shirt again.
12. "Don't fly kites near electric overhead cables," said my father.
    My father _____ me not to fly kites near electric overhead cables.

Exercise 6

Fill the gaps using the verbs in the box in the correct form. Use each verb once only.

add   apologize   explain   promise   admit   beg   offer   protest

1. The teacher _____ that wine came from grapes.
2. He _____ never to take her CDs again without asking first.
3. He _____ for being late.
4. Monica _____ to give us a lift to the station.
5. Mike _____ eating the last chocolate biscuit.
6. Our scoutmaster _____ at the end of his speech that we mustn't forget to bring torches on the camping trip.
7. Cecilia _____ that she couldn't help with the shopping because she had already arranged to meet Caroline.
8. Cinderella _____ to be allowed to go to the ball.

Unit 17　Argument in research papers

17.1　Introduction

When writing research papers, you are not supposed to present the readers merely with facts. You should present them with an informed argument. To construct an informed argument, you must first try to sort out what you *know* about a subject from what you *think* about a subject. Or, to put it another way, you will want to consider what *is known* about a subject and then to determine what *you* think about it. If your paper fails to inform, or if it fails to argue, then it will fail to meet the expectations of the academic reader.

The purpose of argument, in an academic setting, is to analyze an issue or a situation and to make a case for your point of view, to convince your reader or listener of the truth of something. In fact, making an argument — expressing a point of view on a subject and supporting it with evidence — is often the aim of academic writing.

Many people will associate argument with two persons quarrelling with each other. But academic argument is something different. Instead of heated discussion, academic argument is calm. Instead of personal references, academic argument uses impersonal, logical reasons and evidence to make a point.

You will come across argument very often when you are writing your research paper. Actually, most material you read when preparing for your paper is or has been debated by someone, somewhere, at some time. Even when the material is presented as simple "fact", it may actually be one person's interpretation of a set of information. In your writing, you are supposed to question that interpretation and defend it, refute it, or offer some new view of your own. Therefore in writing research papers, you will almost always need to do more than just present information that you have gathered. You will need to select a point of view and provide evidence (in other words, use "argument") to shape the material and offer your interpretation of the material.

17.2　What is an argument?

17.2.1　Components of an argument

In academic writing, an argument is usually a main idea, often called a "claim", an "assertion" or a "thesis statement" backed up with evidence that supports the idea. Whatever you call it, you will need to make some sort of claim and use evidence to support it. In another word, to make a convincing case, academic argument has two elements.

(1) an assertion, e. g. , your argument, or what you are trying to prove (usually crystalized in an essay's thesis sentence);

(2) proof, e. g. , evidence to show the truth of the argument.

17.2.2 Usual mistakes in dealing with arguments

All this sounds very simple: you state your point and back it up. But things can go wrong even at the outset of work when you are constructing your argument. Look at these three aruments:
- X is better than Y.
- Scents in the office can affect people's work.
- UFOs are really government regulated.

Immediately you can see that the middle example, *Scents in the office can affect people's work*, is an argument that can probably be proven. There have been some studies done on the use of scents and their effect on workplace actions, workers' emotions and productivity. It's likely that you will be able to find information on this in scientific or business journals that are written for professionals in those fields. So this might actually be provable in terms of academic argument.

It's hard to determine whether the first example, *X is better than Y*, is provable, as it's not a specific enough assertion. You'd need to define *X* and *Y* precisely, and you'd need to define the term *better* precisely in order even to approach having a provable argument. The point here is that an argument needs to be precise to be provable.

The last example, *UFOs are really government regulated*, may not be provable. *UFO* is a general term that needs to be more precise, as does *government* (whose government?). Even if you define *UFO* and *government*, it may be impossible to find evidence to prove this assertion.

For several reasons things can also go wrong when are trying to back up your assertion (claim) with evidence. Firstly, there are different types of assertions, and you need to choose an assertion that can be proven logically. Secondly, there are also different types of proof that can be used, and you need to choose the appropriate types for your particular case. Thirdly, sometimes even if you have a generally acceptable assertion and appropriate proof, there are lots of ways to influence the argument through language, and you need to choose language that is dispassionate and not too biased so that you're focusing your proof on evidence instead of emotion.

17.2.3 Development of argument

Arguments in academic writing are usually complex and take time to develop. Your argument will need to be more than a simple or obvious statement such as "William Shakespeare is the greatest writer". Such a statement might capture your initial impressions of Shakespeare as you have studied him in class; however, you need to look deeper and express specifically what caused that "greatness". The readers will probably expect something more complicated, such as "William Shakespeare's writing combines elements of foreign legends and locally found materials to create a unique new style", or "There are many strong similarities between Shakespeare's writing and those of his contemporaries, which suggests that he may have borrowed some of their ideas". To develop your argument, you would then define your terms and prove your claim with evidence from William Shakespeare's writings and those of the other writers you mentioned.

17.3 Evidence

Just have a thesis statement in your paper is not enough. You have to back up your point with evidence. The strength of your evidence, and your use of it, can make or break your argument.

Evidence generally falls into two categories: facts and opinions. A "fact" is something that has been demonstrated or verified as true or something that is generally accepted as truth. For example, it's a fact that the world is round. On the other hand, opinion is based upon observation and is not as absolutely verifiable as fact.

Both fact and opinion can be acceptable, logical proof for an academic argument. Many students assume, incorrectly, that the more facts, the better support for an argument; and they try to load the support up with dates or numbers. But the opinions of experts in the field are just as important as facts in constituting evidence for an argument. Expert opinion means that a professional, well-versed in a field, has interpreted and drawn conclusions from whatever facts exist.

Every field has slightly different requirements for acceptable evidence, so familiarize yourself with some arguments from within that field instead of just applying whatever evidence you like best.

Be consistent with your evidence. A research paper is not the place for a collection of every type of argument. You can often use more than one type of evidence within a paper, but make sure that within each section you are providing the reader with evidence appropriate to each claim.

17.4 Relationship between argument and evidence

The assertion and the evidence need to relate to one another carefully and logically to have a solid, acceptable argument. Problems can easily occur in the relationship between assertion and evidence. (see section 2.2)

For example, you can't logically argue that adult students don't like lectures on the basis of interviews with one or two adult students. You can't assume that because this situation is true for one or two adult learners, it's true for all.

You can't logically argue that our weather has changed on the earth because of our forays into outer space. You can't conclude that one action has been the sole cause of another action.

You can't logically argue that we have to be either for or against a proposition. You can't assume that only those two responses exist.

As you can see, you need to be careful in thinking through the relationship between assertion and proof. In general, the assertion and any assumptions underlying the assertion need to be generally acceptable, while the proof needs to be sufficient, relevant to the assertion and free of incorrect assumptions and conclusions.

17.5　Counterargument

One way to strengthen your argument and show that you have a deep understanding of the issue you are discussing is to anticipate and address counterarguments or objections. By considering what someone who disagrees with your position might have to say about your argument, you show that you have thought things through, and you dispose of some of the reasons your audience might have for not accepting your argument.

Once you have thought up some counterarguments, consider how you will respond to them — will you concede that your opponent has a point but explain why your audience should nonetheless accept your argument? Will you reject the counterargument and explain why it is mistaken? Either way, you will want to leave your reader with a sense that your argument is stronger than opposing arguments.

When you are summarizing opposing arguments, present each of them fairly and objectively. You want to show that you have seriously considered the many sides of the issue and that you are not simply attacking your opponents.

It is usually better to consider one or two serious counterarguments in some depth, rather than to give a long but superficial list of many different counterarguments and replies.

Be sure that your reply is consistent with your original argument. If considering a counterargument changes your position, you will need to go back and revise your original argument accordingly.

17.6　The role of audience and language in argument

Audience is a very important consideration in argument. It's usually wise to think of your audience in an academic setting as someone who is perfectly smart but who doesn't necessarily agree with you. You are not just expressing your opinion in an argument, and in most cases your audience will know something about the subject at hand — so you will need sturdy proof. At the same time, do not think of your audience as knowing everything. You have to state both your claim and your evidence clearly.

Language style and use is also crucially important to argument. Has an attempt been made to use straightforward language, or is the language emotionally charged? Has an attempt been made to argue through reliance on evidence, or does the argument rely on swaying your thoughts through word choice and connotation? Is the language precise or vague? Concrete or abstract? Argument exists not only in ideas but also in the way those ideas are presented through language.

17.7 An example of argument in an essay

Now we will look at a paragraph in the body section of an essay to see how a main point is established then supported with evidence from the literature. The paragraph example below develops the point in the example essay that the divisiveness between the states was another major obstacle to national unity. Notice how paraphrased information from source material is used to develop and to provide support for the idea presented in the topic sentence.

Passage with analysis

The divisiveness between the states was another major obstacle to national unity. Despite sharing a common heritage such as the Roman Empire, the Renaissance and Catholicism, many divisions were evident between the Italian states. One example of these divisions was that the majority of the population only spoke the dialect of their own region. In fact, when Italy was unified, only four percent of the population had knowledge of the official Italian language (Duggan, 1994: 156). The enormous differences between the regions were exacerbated by the keen political and commercial rivalry that existed between these states. Guise Mizzen, the leading agitator for the unification of Italy at this period, declared:	topic sentence supporting evidence expansion supporting evidence (quotes a primary source)
We have no flag, no political name, no rank among European nations. We have no common centre, no common fact, no common market. We are dismembered into eight states... all independent of one another, without alliance, without unity of aim, without connection... (these factors) divide us and render us as much possible strangers to each other (1845:36).	
A striking example of the commercial division and rivalry between the states which impeded the national economic interest was the existence of as many as twenty two customs' barriers around the Po River region of Italy (Mack Smith, 1959). In addition to these divisions between the states, mistrust of each other's economic and political motives was also evident.	further supporting evidence transition to next paragraph

Exercise 1

The following appeared in a newspaper story giving advice about investments.

"As overall life expectancy continues to rise, the population of our country is growing increasingly older. For example, over twenty percent of the residents of one of our more populated regions are now at least 65 years old, and occupancy rates at resort hotels in that region declined significantly during the past six months. Because of these two related trends, a prudent investor would be well-advised to sell interest in hotels and invest in hospitals and nursing homes instead."

Discuss how well reasoned the argument is.

Sample answer

In this argument prudent investors are advised to stop investing in hotels and invest instead in hospitals and nursing homes. The author cites two related trends — an aging population and a decline in hotel occupancy — as grounds for this advice. To illustrate these trends, the author refers to another region of the country, where 20 percent of the population is over 65 years old and where occupancy rates in resort hotels have declined significantly during the past six months. This argument is unconvincing in a couple of important respects.

In the first place, the author provides no evidence to support the claim that the population as a whole is aging and that the hotel occupancy rate in general is declining. The example cited, while suggestive of these trends, is insufficient to warrant their truth because ...

In the second place, the author has provided no evidence to support the claim that the decline in hotel occupancy is related to the aging of the population. The author appears to believe that the decrease in occupancy rates at resort hotels is somehow caused by the increase in the number of people over age 65. ...

In conclusion, the author's investment advice is not based on sound reasoning. To strengthen the conclusion, the author must show that the trends were not restricted to a particular region of the country. The author must also show that the cause of the decline in hotel occupancy is the increase in the number of people over 65.

Exercise 2

The following appeared as part of an annual report sent to stockholders by Olympic Foods, a processor of frozen foods.

"Over time, the costs of processing go down because as organizations learn how to do things better, they become more efficient. In color film processing, for example, the cost of a 3-by-5-inch print fell from 50 cents for five-day service in 1970 to 20 cents for one-day service in 1984. The same principle applies to the processing of food. And since Olympic Foods will soon celebrate its twenty-fifth birthday, we can expect that our long experience will enable us to minimize costs and thus maximize profits."

Discuss how well reasoned you find this argument.

Exercise 3

Discuss how well reasoned the argument in the following passage is.

"Last year, the city contracted with Flower Power to plant a variety of flowers in big decorative pots on Main Street and to water them each week. By midsummer many of the plants were wilted. This year the city should either contract for two waterings a week or save money by planting artificial flowers in the pots. According to Flower Power, the initial cost for artificial flowers would be twice as much as for real plants, but after two years, we would save money. Public reaction certainly supports this position: in a recent survey, over 1 200 Gazette readers said that the city wastes money and should find ways to reduce spending."

Unit 18　The Harvard style of referencing

18.1　Introduction

18.1.1　Definition of citation and referencing

During the course of writing a research paper, it is usual to support arguments by reference to other published work. These references may be from work presented in journal or newspaper articles, government reports, books or specific chapters of books, research dissertations or theses, material from the Internet etc.

Citation is the practice of referring to the work of other authors in the text of your own piece of work. Such works are cited to show evidence both of the background reading that has been done and to support the content and conclusions. Each citation requires a reference at the end of the work.

Reference gives the full details of the source item and should enable it to be traced. Referring accurately to such source materials is part of sound academic practice and a skill that should be mastered. Other reasons for accurate citation and referencing are:
- to give credit to the concepts and ideas of other authors;
- to provide the reader with evidence of the breadth and depth of your reading;
- to enable those who read your work to locate the cited references easily.

18.1.2　Plagiarism

Plagiarism is the submission of an item of assessment containing elements of work produced by another person(s) in such a way that it could be assumed to be the student's own work. Examples of plagiarism are:
- the copying of another person's work without acknowledgement;
- the close paraphrasing of another person's work without acknowledgement;
- the unacknowledged quotation of phrases from another person's work.

Copying or close paraphrasing with occasional acknowledgement of the source may also be deemed to be plagiarism if the absence of quotation marks implies that the phraseology is the student's own.

18.1.3　Referencing systems

There are a number of systems for the citation of references. The writer of this book expects students to use the alphabetical/name-date system, in a particular style, known as the HARVARD style. In this style, the author's surname and year of publication are cited in the text, e.g. (Bond, 2004) and a reference list (of these citations) is included at the end of the assignment, in alphabetical order by author with date. This **reference list** also includes important details such as the title and publisher. A **bibliography** lists relevant items that you have used in the preparation of the assignment but not necessarily cited in your text. A bibliography should also be in the Harvard style and the inclusion of such a list shows that you have read widely beyond the items you have cited.

18.2　Citing references in text using the Harvard system

References to sources may be cited in the text in different ways depending on the nature of the sentence/paragraph that is being written.

18.2.1　Author's name cited in the text

When making reference to an author's work in your text, their name is followed by the year of publication of their work, and page reference, in brackets (parentheses) and forms part of the sentence:

Cormack (1994, pp.32-33) states that "when writing for a professional readership, writers invariably make reference to already published works".

In general, when writing for a professional publication, it is good practice to make reference to other relevant published work. This view has been supported in the work of Cormack (1994, pp.32-33).

18.2.2　Author's name not cited directly in the text

If you make reference to a work or piece of research without mentioning the author in the text then both the author's name and publication year are placed at the relevant point in the sentence or at the end of the sentence in brackets:

Making reference to published work appears to be characteristic of writing for a professional audience (Cormack, 1994).

18.2.3　More than one author cited in the text

Where reference is made to more than one author in a sentence, and they are referred to directly, they are both cited:

Jones (1946) and Smith (1948) have both shown...

18.2.4　More than one author not cited directly in the text

List these at the relevant point in the sentence or at the end of the sentence, putting the author's name, followed by the date of publication and separated by a semi-colon and within brackets:

Further research in the late forties (Jones, 1946; Smith, 1948) lead to major developments...

18.2.5　Two authors for the same work

When there are two authors for a work they should both be noted in the text:

White and Brown (1964) in their recent research paper found...

Earlier research (White & Brown, 1966) demonstrated that the presence of certain chemicals would lead to...

18.2.6　More than two authors for a work

Where there are several authors (more than two), only the first author should be used, followed by "**et al.**" meaning "and others":

Green, et al. (1995) found that the majority ...

or indirectly:

Recent research has found that the majority of... (Green, et al., 1995)

18.2.7　Page numbers

Including the page numbers of a reference will help readers trace your sources. This is particularly important for quotations and for paraphrasing specific paragraphs in the texts:

Lawrence (1966, p. 124)

or indirectly:

(Lawrence, 1966, p. 124)

18.2.8　Several works by one author in different years

If more than one publication from an author illustrates the same point and the works are published in different years, then the references should be cited in chronological order (i.e. earliest first):

as suggested by Bloggs (1992, 1994)

or indirectly:

(Bloggs 1992, 1994)...

18.2.9　Several works by one author in the same year

If you are quoting several works published by the same author in the same year, they should be differentiated by adding a lower case letter after the year for each item:

Earlier research by Smith (1993a) found that... but later research suggested again by Smith (1993b) that...

18.2.10　Secondary sources (second-hand references)

While you are consulting an original work, you may come across a summary of another author's work, which you would like to make reference to in your own document. This is called secondary referencing.

A direct reference:

Research recently carried out by Brown (1966 cited in Bassett, 1986, p. 142) found that...

In this example, Brown is the work which you wish to refer to, but have not read directly for yourself. Bassett is the secondary source, where you found the summary of Brown's work.

Or indirectly:

(Brown, 1966 cited in Bassett, 1986, p. 142)

18.3 Compiling the reference list and bibliography

18.3.1 General guidelines, layout and punctuation

The purpose of a reference list is to enable sources to be easily traced by another reader. Different types of publication require different amounts of information but there are certain common elements such as authorship, year of publication and title.

The Harvard style lays down standards for the order and content of information in the reference. Some variations of layout are acceptable provided that they are used consistently.

All items should be listed alphabetically by author or authorship, regardless of the format, i.e. whether books, websites or journal articles etc. Where there are several works from one author or source they should by listed together but in date order with the earliest work listed first.

18.3.2 Books

Use the title page, not the book cover, for the reference details. The required elements for a book reference are:

Author, Initials/First name., Year. *Title of book*. Edition. Place of publication: Publisher.

Redman, P., 2006. *Good essay writing: a social sciences guide*. 3rd ed. London: Open University in assoc. with Sage.

Baron, David P., 2008. *Business and the organisation*. 6th ed. Chester (CT): Pearson.

18.3.2.1 Books with two, three or four authors

For books with two, three or four authors of equal status the names should all be included in the order they appear in the document. Use an ampersand (&) to link the last two multiple authors.

The required elements for a reference are:

Authors, Initials., Year. *Title of book*. Edition. (only include this if not the first edition) Place: Publisher.

Barker, R. Kirk, J. & Munday, R. J., 1988. *Narrative analysis*. 3rd ed. Bloomington: Indiana University Press.

18.3.2.2 Books with more than four authors

For books where there are more than four authors, use the first author only with surname and initials followed by et al.

The required elements for a reference are:

Author, Initials., Year. *Title of book*. Edition. (only include this if not the first edition) Place: Publisher.

Grace, B. et al., 1988. *A history of the world*. Princeton, NJ: Princeton University Press.

18.3.2.3 Books which are edited

For books which are edited give the editor(s) surname(s) and initials, followed by ed. or eds.

The required elements for a reference are:

Author, Initials., Year. *Title of book.* Edition. (only include this if not the first edition) Place of publication: Publisher.

Keene, E. ed., 1988. *Natural language.* Cambridge: University of Cambridge Press.

18.3.2.4 Multiple works by the same author

Where there are several works by one author and published in the same year they should be differentiated by adding a lower case letter after the date.

For multiple works the required elements for a reference are:

Author, Year. *Title of book.* Place of publication: Publisher.

Soros, G., 1966a. *The road to serfdom.* Chicago: University of Chicago Press.

Soros, G., 1966b. *Beyond the road to serfdom.* Chicago: University of Chicago Press.

18.3.2.5 Books which have been translated

For works which have been translated the reference should include details of the translator, the suggested elements for such references are:

Author, Year. *Title of book.* Translated from (language) by (name of translator) Place of publication: Publisher.

Canetti, E., 2001. *The voices of Marrakesh: a record of a visit.* Translated from German by J. A. Underwood. San Francisco: Arion.

18.3.3 Journal articles and newspapers

18.3.3.1 Journal articles

For journal articles the required elements for a reference are:

Author, Initials., Year. Title of article. *Full Title of Journal*, Volume number (Issue/Part number), Page numbers.

Boughton, J.M., 2002. The Bretton Woods proposal: an in-depth look. *Political Science Quarterly*, 42 (6), pp.564-578.

Perry, C., 2001. What health care assistants know about clean hands. *Nursing Times*, 25 May, 97 (22), pp.63-64.

18.3.3.2 Journal articles from an electronic source

For journal articles from an electronic source the required elements for a reference are:

Author, Initials., Year. Title of article. *Full Title of Journal*, [type of medium] Volume number (Issue/Part number), Page numbers if available.

Available at: include web site address/URL (Uniform Resource Locator) and additional details of access, such as the routing from the home page of the source. [Accessed date].

Boughton, J.M., 2002. The Bretton Woods proposal: an in-depth look. *Political Science Quarterly*, [Online]. 42 (6), Available at: Blackwell Science Synergy http://www.pol.upenn/articles [Accessed 12

June 2005].

18.3.3.3 Newspaper articles

For newspaper articles the required elements for a reference are:

Author, Initials. , Year. Title of article. *Full Title of Newspaper*, Day and month before page number and column line.

Slapper, G. , 2005. Corporate manslaughter: new issues for lawyers. *The Times*, 3 Sep. p. 4b.

18.4 Websites

For websites found on the world wide web the required elements for a reference are:

Authorship or Source, Year. *Title of web document or web page*. [Medium] (date of update) Available at: include web site address/URL (Uniform Resource Locator) and additional details such as access or routing from the home page of the source. [Accessed date].

National Electronic Library for Health, 2003. *Can walking make you slimmer and healthier?* (Hitting the headlines article) [Online] (Updated 16 Jan. 2005) Available at: http://www.nhs.uk.hth.walking [Accessed 10 April 2005].

18.5 The Harvard and APA referencing systems

The most common referencing systems are the Harvard and American Psychological Association (APA) systems. The Harvard and APA systems are very similar, since they are both reference information by providing the surname of the author, the year and the page number(s) in the text of the essay. All the bibliographic information (title, edition, place, publisher) appears in a list of references at the end of the essay.

18.5.1 Differences between Harvard and APA in-text referencing

In the text of your essay, the APA style is specified as:
- *APA style*: (Apple, 2000, p. 15)

However, the Harvard style is less prescriptive about the way a reference is written, for example:
- *Harvard style*: (Apple 2000:15) or (Apple 2000, 15)

Particular disciplines or departments may require you to use a specific style when referencing, such as the APA preferred style of writing a reference. However, you aren't likely to lose marks if you use a comma, instead of a colon. The rule of thumb is to choose the style that you prefer and to use it consistently throughout your essay. If you are unsure what is the most common style to use in your discipline, ask your lecturer, refer to a style guide (if available) or use a major journal in your discipline as a basic guide.

18.5.2 Differences between the Harvard and APA reference list formats

The main difference between the Harvard and APA systems is in their reference list formats. An example of a Harvard reference list is given below:

- Apple, A. N. (2000) *Sociology Today*, Sydney: Allen & Unwin.
- Apple, A. N. (1993) 'Culture and change', *Social Theory*, Vol. 5, No. 2, 1-10.
- Orang, O. (1999) *History Tomorrow*, Sydney: Allen & Unwin.

The APA system places full-stops after titles, doesn't use quotation marks for chapter or article titles, and writes the volume number differently to the Harvard system. (Note that there is no issue number included for APA.) The same example using the APA system would look as follows:

- Apple, A. N. (2000) *Sociology Today.* Sydney: Allen & Unwin.
- Apple, A. N. (1993) Culture and change. *Social Theory*, 5, 1 - 10.
- Orang, O. (1999) *History Tomorrow.* Sydney: Allen & Unwin.

Exercise 1

Fill in the table below using the information from the references given.

Alderson, J. C. (2001). *Assessing reading.* Cambridge: Cambridge University Press.

American Psychological Association (2001). *Publication manual of the American Psychological Association* (5th ed.). Washington, D C: American Psychological Association.

Bazerman, C. (1989). *Shaping written knowledge.* Madison, W I: University of Wisconsin Press.

Bell, J. (1999). *Doing your research project.* Buckingham: Open University Press.

Benesch, S. (2001). *Critical English for academic purposes.* Malwah, N J: Lawrence Erlbaum Associates.

Bex, T. (1996). *Variety in written English.* London: Routledge.

Herbert, A. J. (1965). *The structure of technical English.* London: Longman.

Lillis, T. M. (2001). *Student writing: Access, regulation, desire.* London: Routledge.

McCarthy, M. & Carter, R. (1994). *Language as discourse.* London: Longman.

Ramsden, P. (1992). *Learning to teach in higher education.* London: Routledge.

Swales, J. (1998). *Other floors, other voices.* Mahwah, N J: Lawrence Erlbaum.

	Author	Title of book	Place of publication	Publisher	Date
e.g.	J. C. Alderson	Assessing reading	Cambridge	Cambridge University Press	2001
1					
2					
3					
4					
5					
6					

	Author	Title of book	Place of publication	Publisher	Date
7					
8					
9					
10					

Exercise 2

Fill in the table below using the information from the references given.

Abo Mosallem, E. (1984). English for police officers in Egypt. *English for Specific Purposes*, 3, 171-182.

Bayne, B. L. (1972). Some effects of stress in the adult on the larval development of Mytilus edulis. *Nature*, 237, 459-475.

Becher, T. (1981). Towards a definition of disciplinary cultures. *Studies in Higher Education*, 6, 109-122.

Belcher, D. (1989). How professors initiate non-native speakers into their disciplinary discourse communities. *Texas Papers in Foreign Language Education*, 1, 207-225.

Cummings, T. G. (1978). Self-regulating work groups: A socio-technical synthesis. *Academy of Management Review*, 3, 625-634.

Fitzgerald, J. (1990). The misconceived revolution: State and society in China's nationalist revolution, 1923-1926. *Journal of Asian Studies*, 49, 323-343.

Hallin, D. C. (1992). Sound Bite News: Television Coverage of Elections, 1968-1988. *Journal of Communication*, 42, 5-24.

Harris, S. & Ghauri, P. (2000). Strategy formation by business leaders: Exploring the influence of national values. *European Journal of Marketing*, 34, 126-142.

Hyltenstam, K. (1977). Implicational patterns in interlanguage syntax variation. *Language Learning*, 27, 383-411.

Sillince, J. A. A. (1995). Extending the cognitive approach to strategic change in organizations: Some theory. *British Journal of Management*, 6, 59-76.

Tuckman, B. W. (1965). Developmental sequences in small groups. *Psychological Bulletin*, 63, 384-399.

	Author	Title of article	Title of journal	Journal volume	Page numbers	Date
e.g.	E. Abo Mosallem	English for police officers in Egypt	English for Specific Purposes	3	171-182	1984
1						
2						

	Author	Title of article	Title of journal	Journal volume	Page numbers	Date
3						
4						
5						
6						
7						
8						
9						
10						

Exercise 3

Distinguish between books and journals in the following list.

1. Abo Mosallem, E. (1984). English for police officers in Egypt. *English for Specific Purposes*, 3, 171-182.
2. Alderson, J. C. (2001). *Assessing reading*. Cambridge: Cambridge University Press.
3. Alderson, J. C. & Urquhart, A. H. (1985). The effect of students' academic discipline on their performance on ESP reading tests. *Language Testing*, 2, 192-204.
4. Anderson, P. L. (1986). English for academic listening: Teaching the skills associated with listening to extended discourse. *Foreign Language Annals*, 19, 391-397.
5. Arden-Close, C. (1993). Language problems in science lectures to non-native speakers. *English for Specific Purposes*, 12, 251-261.
6. Atkinson, D. & Ramanathan, V. (1995). Cultures of writing: An ethnographic comparison of L1 and L2 university writing/language programs. *TESOL Quarterly*, 29, 539-568.
7. Barton, D., Hamilton, M. & Ivanic, R. (Eds.). (2000). *Situated literacies: Reading and writing in context*. London: Routledge.
8. Bates, M. & Dudley-Evans, T. (1976). *Nucleus — General Science*. London: Longman.
9. Batstone, R. (1988). Teachers and course design: The case for a modular approach. *ELT Journal*, 42, 185-195.
10. Bazerman, C. (1989). *Shaping written knowledge*. Madison, WI: University of Wisconsin Press.
11. Becher, T. (1981). Towards a definition of disciplinary cultures. *Studies in Higher Education*, 6, 109-122.
12. Becher, T. (1989). *Academic tribes and territories: Intellectual enquiry and the culture of disciplines*. Buckingham: The Society for Research into Higher Education and Open University Press.

13. Belcher, D. (1989). How professors initiate non-native speakers into their disciplinary discourse communities. *Texas Papers in Foreign Language Education*, 1, 207-225.

Exercise 4

Put the following in alphabetical order.

1. Wong, R., Glendinning, E. & Mantell, H. (1994). *Becoming a writer.* London: Longman.
2. Walker, T. (1992). *English for academic purposes — computer science.* London: Prentice Hall.
3. Yates, C. St. J. (1992). *English for academic purposes — Agriculture.* London: Prentice Hall.
4. Zimmerman, F. (1989). *English for science.* London: Prentice Hall.
5. Carol, B. J. & West, R. (1989). *ESU framework: Performance scales for English language examinations.* London: Longman.
6. Chafe, W. (1982). Integration and involvement in speaking, writing, and oral literature. In D. Tannen (Ed.), *Spoken and written language: Exploring orality and literacy.* Norwood, NJ: Ablex Publishing Corporation.
7. Cookson, L. (1984). *Writing.* London: Hutchinson.
8. Davies, A., & Criper, C. (1987). *Research report 1: ELTS validation project report.* Edinburgh: University of Edinburgh.
9. Ferguson, N. & O'Reilly, M. (1977). *Listening and note taking.* London: Evans.
10. Murphy, R. (1985). *English grammar in use.* Oxford: Oxford University Press.
11. Hogue, A. (1996). *First steps in academic writing.* London: Longman.
12. International English Language Testing System (1989). *An Introduction to IELTS.* London: The British Council.
13. Laird, E. (1977). *English in focus: English in education.* Oxford: Oxford University Press.
14. Jones, L. (1981). *Functions of English.* Cambridge: Cambridge University Press.
15. Northedge, A. (1990). *The good study guide.* Milton Keynes: The Open University Press.
16. Davies, E. & Whitney, N. (1981). *Strategies for reading.* London: Heinemann.
17. O'Connor, J. D. (1980). *Better English pronunciation* (new ed.). Cambridge: Cambridge University Press.
18. Alderson, J. C., Krahnke, K. J. & Standfield, C. W. (Eds.). (1987). *Reviews of English language proficiency tests.* Washington, DC: TESOL.
19. Pirie, D. B. (1985). *How to write critical essays.* London: Routledge.
20. Davies, S. & West, R. (1984). *The Pitman Guide To English Language Examinations* (2nd ed.). London: Pitman.

Keys

Unit 1 What is research?

Exercise 1

1. What is research?

Research is a process through which we attempt to achieve systematically and with the support of data the answer to a question, the solution to a problem, or a greater understanding of a phenomenon.

2. What are the features of research?

Research originates with a question or problem.
Research requires a clear expression of a goal.
Research requires a specific plan of procedure.
Research usually divides the principal problem into more manageable subproblems.
Research is guided by the specific research problem, question, or hypothesis.
Research requires the collection and interpretation of data.
Research is, by its nature, cyclical.

3. What do we mean by the statement "research is cyclical"?

Research is never conclusive. In another word, the "circle of research" might be more accurately thought of as a spiral of research. In exploring an area, one comes across additional problems that need resolving. One research leads to another research. Every researcher soon learns that genuine research creates more problems than it resolves. Such is the nature of the discovery of knowledge.

4. What methods do we often use in doing research?

Research methods can be various, the following are the most frequently used: questionnaires, observations, interviews and eliciting.

Exercise 2

1. The bulb has burned out.
2. The lamp is not plugged into the wall outlet.
3. A late afternoon thunderstorm interrupted the electrical service.
4. The wire from the lamp to the wall outlet is defective.
5. You forgot to pay your electric bill.

Unit 2 What is a research paper?

Exercise 1

1. Abstract
2. Introduction
3. Methods

4. Results

5. Discussion

Exercise 2

(Answers may vary according to the different articles students read.)

Unit 3 Features of effective writing

Exercise 1

1. A 2. C 3. B 4. I 5. D 6. E 7. G 8. H 9. F 10. J

Exercise 2

A.

Exercise 3

Working women who must travel on their own.

Exercise 4

Passage 1

It's difficult to identify babies' earliest spoken language.

Passage 2

Successfully transplanting a tree requires careful attention to details.

Exercise 5

Passage 1 some problems with these machines

Passage 2 some pieces of advice are certainly needed

Unit 4 Features of academic writing

Exercise 1

1.

It may be said...

2.

...it may be possible...

3.

...seem...

Exercise 2

The first paragraph is more objective.

Exercise 3

	Informal	Formal
1	Everybody must...	It is essential/crucial/vital that all parties...
2	In our daily lives we experience the influence of...	Daily life is influenced by...
3	We simply/just order goods from...	Goods can be ordered directly from...
4	Let us consider...	It is important to consider...
5	It's high time we all did the right thing.	The current situation requires action from all citizens...
6	We can't see and touch the goods.	Goods cannot be seen or touched...
7	When we download songs we cheat their authors of income.	Downloading songs infringes on the interests of their authors.
8	We, Chinese, do things our own way.	Chinese people tend to do things in a certain way.
9	I love/ I like/ prefer...	Personally, I favour...
10	We face a huge danger of being cheated...	There is a serious risk of fraud...
11	You may ask...	One may ask...
12	Students have their own styles of learning...	Students learn in different ways...
13	We can do many things...	Many things can be done/are possible...

Exercise 4

	Informal	Formal
1	Life is not a rose garden. Life is tough.	Life presents a number of challenges.
2	On top of that...	Another point is that...
3	In a nutshell...	To state it briefly / In brief,...
4	Last but not least...	A final and equally/very important point is...
5	Government must make laws...	There is a need for laws...
6	Hong Kong is an international city, so we all must...	The trend of globalisation makes it necessary for many people to...
7	Every coin has two sides.	There are advantages and disadvantages to...
8	By the way...	Incidentally...
9	Pros & cons of...	The points for and against...
10	Government & the people must join hands together...	Cooperation between the Government and the public is vital...

Exercise 5

1. investigating   2. raised   3. intervene   4. eliminate   5. reduced   6. establish
7. fluctuate   8. proposed

Exercise 6
1. tolerate 2. caused 3. considering 4. fall 5. continued 6. canceled 7. demolished 8. reduced

Exercise 7
1. considerable 2. obtained 3. numerous 4. consequences 5. extremely 6. arising from

Exercise 8
1. fairly 2. promising 3. meeting 4. helpful 5. events 6. fired 7. wonderful

Exercise 9
1. were not 2. will 3. has 4. is 5. are not 6. does not 7. would rather 8. did not

Exercise 10
1. The same theory of learning can be applied to small children.
2. This can only be done after the initial preparation has been conducted.
3. The figures are accurate to within 1%, but the application of local variations should be noted.
4. In the second section of the report, the environmental consequences will be taken into consideration.

Exercise 11
1. In this essay, the main differences between the English and Scottish legal systems will be discussed.
2. My report has been divided into five sections.
3. The conclusion proposes that all drugs should be legalized.
4. This essay argues that the importance of the monarchy should be reduced.
5. The reasons for public hysteria over the SARS virus will be discussed in the third part of the essay.
6. Great effort has been made to understand the main ideas.

Exercise 12
1. Today many people use credit cards for their shopping.
2. Drinking wine can be bad for you.
3. Global warming might have disastrous consequences for the whole world.
4. Teleworking may lead to isolation.
5. Some women tend to be worse drivers than men.

Exercise 13

1. The positive feedback compensated for problems incurred during the trial.
2. The difference between these two leaning processes is easily visible / apparent/ evident.
3. The study participants completed the task without any difficulty.
4. Many examples of autonomous systems are found in a lot of countries.

Unit 5 Steps in writing a research paper

Exercise 1

Revision is the final step to take before you finish writing your research paper. The goals for revision are, first, to examine the paper to find out mistakes in the writing; second, to enable an effective an accurate presentation of ideas; and thirdly, to make the paper as good as it can be by making certain that the arguments are strong and the written expression is accurate.

Exercise 2

Aerobic exercise is good for your health.
Drunk driving is hazardous.

Exercise 3

Answers may vary according to the different interests of the students.

Exercise 4

Thesis B.

Exercise 5

Number 1 is the summary; it has condensed the source and articulates the main idea. Number 2 is an appropriate paraphrase. The writer has used her own words and sentence structure to relate the essence of the source.

Unit 6 Developing an outline

Exercise 1

The College Application Process

I   Choose Desired Colleges
   A. Visit and evaluate college campuses
   B. Visit and evaluate college websites
     1. look for interesting classes
     2. note important statistics
       a. student/faculty ratio
       b. retention rate

II. Prepare Application
   A. Write personal statement
      1. Choose interesting topic
         Describe an influential person in your life
         （1）favorite high school teacher
         （2）grandparent
      2. Include important personal details
         a. volunteer work
         b. participation in varsity sports
   B. Revise personal statement

III. Compile resume
   A. List relevant coursework
   B. List work experience
   C. List volunteer experience
      1. tutor at foreign language summer camp
      2. counselor for suicide prevention hotline

Exercise 2

Topic: Benefits of Distant Learning

Outline:

I. Distance Learning is very easy, easier than one might expect.
   A. Do not dread distance learning. It is not complicated at all. In fact, it is very easy since new technological advancements have made it very easy and user friendly for people.
   B. Communication has been made very easy these days. People can talk at a touch of a button. No need for complicated machinery.
   C. The teachers and students can communicate with each other very easily by e-mails, print data and video conferencing is also possible. None of this requires any special training. Even children can do these tasks!
   D. There is no need to buy and install any sort of complicated machinery or hardware. Teachers as well as students can use their normal home computers to interact with each other over large distances.

II. Benefits of distance learning.
   A. Learn and teach from the leisure and ease of your home.
   B. Both teachers as well as students can talk to each other at any time.
   C. Is not expensive at all; as low as half the price of normal education.
   D. Research has concluded that it can be made as effective as normal education. Some people argue that it can even be better than going to normal schools.

III. Conclusion
   A. Distance learning is more future-oriented.

B. Students can choose from a variety of courses.
C. A lot of information available online.

Unit 7 Writing academic paragraphs

Exercise 1
1. Adventure tourism is a different way for tourists to see New Zealand.
2. To be successful at university, students need to learn good time-management skills.
3. Obviously the human heart is a small yet highly efficient piece of equipment.

Exercise 2
1. The rapid growth of the world's human population is the most important problem the world needs to address.
2. The Aztecs of Mexico were a nation of accomplished farmers.

Exercise 3
1. Student success at university is the result of a number of inter-related factors.
2. Whether genetic engineering indeed has the benefits promised for us all without the dangers remains open, but it is certainly here to stay.

Exercise 4
1. d f c a b e
2. d a f e g b c

Exercise 5
(1) but (2) however (3) and (4) but (5) so (6) but (7) because

Exercise 6
When **surnames** began ... A **surname** was ... The **names** Walker, ... One of the few occupational **surnames** reflecting ...

Exercise 7
Of course, sometimes they can not go out because of their health. They may have arthritis or rheumatism and it is painful for them to move around. This can also limit their lifestyle.

Exercise 8
1.
Topic sentence:
Year by year more students are borrowing money for their education, and they are borrowing more money.
Evidence in support of topic sentence:

In the first year of the loan scheme 45 000 students had loans. By 1999 the number had grown to 300 000. Two years ago, the average loan debt was NZ $5 000. It is now $10 600, according to figures supplied by the Alliance Party

Source of evidence:

(Gordon, 1999).

Writer's comments:

The total levels of student debt have reached unsustainable levels for the New Zealand economy.

2.

Topic sentence:

It now appears that many students are leaving New Zealand to escape their student loan repayments.

Restatement of topic with more specific detail:

This is particularly acute as a problem in the information technology field.

Evidence in support of topic sentence:

A computer company director has recently reported that graduates who work in his company leave New Zealand after working for only one or two years and that "when we do the exit interview, we find that they're leaving not just because they believe they can get more money, but to escape paying back the student loans."

Source of evidence:

(Gifford, 1999, July 28, p. C1).

Writer's comments:

Surely the government will have to address this problem urgently, especially if the problem is widespread.

Exercise 9

"It may take a militarily powerful nation to establish a language, but it takes an economically powerful one to maintain and expand it" (Crystal, 1997, p. 7).

Exercise 10

1. Concluding paragraph
2. Body paragraph
3. Introductory paragraph
4. Body paragraph

Exercise 11

1. This is the introductory paragraph, giving the background to the essay and specifying its focus.
2. This paragraph outlines some of the claimed economic benefits.
3. This and the following paragraph critique the point of view expressed in the previous

paragraph and disclose the negative effects of tourism on the country's economic wellbeing. This paragraph considers the issues of ownership and control of the industry.
4. This paragraph continues to critique the point of view that tourism brings substantial benefits to the Cook Islands economy. It considers the claim that the creation of jobs is one of the positive side effects of tourism in the Cook Islands.
5. This paragraph is about the claimed social benefits of tourism.
6. This is the concluding paragraph, providing a summary of the argument and recommendations.

Unit 8　What is an abstract?

Exercise 1

1.
Objective:
The basis of this project was to create a garment using mixed media in order to mimic the human body.
Method:
The materials we used to create this piece include: buckram, copper wire, spray paint, fabric paint, a variety of novelty fabrics, and chains. The techniques we created in order to manipulate the piece include: fabric branding and burning, grid painting, sewing, draping, molding buckram, and coiling. Our overall approach was to create a theatrical wearable art piece.
Result and conclusion:
Upon completion of the assignment we found the piece aesthetically pleasing because of the way it molds to the human body, but can be a piece all on its own.

2.
Objective:
The purpose of this study is to identify relationships between the physical and genetic characteristics of bones in mice.
Method:
The physical characteristics include size, density, and the force required to break the bone, while the genetic ones are the genes of the marker loci associated with the genes that affect these qualities. This study uses strains of mice with reduced genetic variation. The two strains of mice that are the most phenotypically extreme, meaning those with the strongest and weakest bones, are crossed. The F2 generation from that cross is then analyzed.
Result and conclusion:
The results of this analysis can be used to find which genotypes correlate with specific bone properties like size, density, and failure load. The anticipated outcome of this lab is the identification of the genotypes that affect bone strength in mice.

The findings may be useful in treating medical conditions that are related to bone strength.

3.

Objective:

This project involves discovering how the American Revolution was remembered during the nineteenth century. The goal is to show that the American Revolution was memorialized by the actions of the United States government during the 1800s.

Method:

This has been done by examining events such as the Supreme Court cases of John Marshall and the Nullification Crisis.

Result and conclusion:

Upon examination of these events, it becomes clear that John Marshall and John Calhoun (creator of the Doctrine of Nullification) attempted to use the American Revolution to bolster their claims by citing speeches from Founding Fathers.

Through showing that the American Revolution lives on in memory, this research highlights the importance of the revolution in shaping the actions of the United States government.

4.

Objective:

The study is to show how even a "sport" video game can incorporate many types of learning, to call attention to what might be overlooked as significant forms of learning, and to understand and take advantage of the opportunities video games afford as more deliberate learning environments.

Method:

The aspects explored are the skills and techniques required to be successful in the game, the environment that skaters skate in, the personal vs. group identity that is shown through the general appearance of the skater, and the values and icons that the game teaches players.

Result and conclusion:

We are finding that sport video games support learning; we hope to find how one learns about oneself as a learner from playing.

5.

Objective:

The greatest obstacle to the development of policies for the curtailment of gender bias is lack of information on the scope and effects of the problem. This study represents an attempt to quantify attitudes toward gender bias among profession women engineers working in the State of Kuwait.

Method:

The major findings that emerged were as follows: a) Since 1970, Kuwait has witnessed an enormous growth rate in the participation of women in higher education. b) With respect to the job-related factors of salary scale, professional treatment, responsibility, benefits, and vacation, a clear majority (68%) of the professional Kuwaiti women engineers surveyed expressed a feeling of equality with or even superiority to their male counterparts. c) The one job-related factor in which significant gender bias was found to be in operation was that of promotion to upper management positions.

Result and conclusion:

In this criterion, the women engineers surveyed felt "less than equal" to their male colleagues.

6.

Objective:

The purpose of this study was to determine the status of the health appraisal services provided for primary school children in Edo State, Nigeria.

Method:

Using the cross-sectional survey design a total of 1506 primary school children were selected from across the state as the study participants. The analysis of data collected through a 14-item questionnaire showed that: four vital aspects of health observation (observation of mouth and teeth, nose and throat, skin, and ears) were not provided for the children; all aspects of health examination were not provided for the children; and records of the health histories of the children were not kept.

Result and conclusion:

These results were discussed and the study recommended that professional counselors be enlisted in the schools for a better management of school health services.

Exercise 2

Purpose:

The purpose of this research is to find out some main principles, translation strategies and skills to guide Chinese-English (C-E) translation of public signs so that the informative and vocative functions of such texts can be fulfilled.

Theoretical basis:

The theoretical basis of this thesis came from Newmark (2001). Newmark points out three main functions of language, namely the expressive, informative and vocative functions, and argues that informative and vocative texts should be communicatively translated. Considering that the chief functions of public signs are informative and vocative, the study concluded that the communicative translation approach should be adopted in translating such texts.

Methodology:

This research was based on field corpus study, surveys and qualitative analysis. The author investigated many bilingual public signs and collected a number of them as samples to be critically analyzed. Besides, ten translations of public signs were selected and transcribed for the questionnaire, which was administered to a group of native English speakers to test their communicative effect. The study found out that translators of public signs are inclined to adopt literal translation, neglecting the communicative function of the source text.

Findings:

On the basis of corpus study, the thesis discovered some most common types of translation mistakes. The research also found out that in order to achieve communicative effect, the translation of public signs should conform to the conventions of English public signs, such as shortness in length, plainness in vocabulary and simplicity in sentence structure. The present research is significant in that it yields some important findings regarding the problems existing in the C-E translation of public signs and offers some feasible solutions to these problems.

Unit 9   Introduction for a research paper

Exercise 1

Move 1:

Show that the research area is important, interesting, problematic, or relevant in some way.

Introduce and review items of previous research and theory in the area.

Move 2:

Indicate a gap in the previous research, raise a question about it, or extend previous knowledge.

Move 3:

Outline purposes or stating the nature of the present research.

Exercise 2

The students can do this by themselves. A sample answer of the first one is given.

In recent research there has been growing interest in economic integration, economic growth and governance.

Exercise 3

The students can do this by themselves. A sample answer of the first one is given.

However, previous research in this field has only concentrated on the application of the theory in translation.

Nevertheless, these attempts to establish a link between secondary smoke and lung cancer are at present controversial.

Exercise 4

The students can do this by themselves. A sample answer of the first one is given.

The aim of the present paper is to give some new definitions of culture.

Exercise 5

This introduction gives a little relevant background and context, indicating that the writer has thought about what a stereotype is in its broadest interpretation; makes some initial references to sources; and finally focuses precisely on the question, showing the reader that it has been fully understood and that it will be answered.

Unit 10   Writing a literature review

Exercise 1
Sequence: chronological order
Sources:
Coates (1988)
Lakoff's (1975)
Maltz and Borker (1982)
Tannen (1987)
Cameron, McAlinden and O'Leary (1988)
Zimmerman and West (1975)

Unit 11   Conclusion

Exercise 1
Conclusion 1
Many trees every day are cut down in the rainforest due to logging. Every day more people are born and new houses built. In only a few years many species may become extinct forever. The deforestation causes the earth to get warmer which can affect all species on the earth. People are helping to stop it, but rainforest destruction still continues. The traditional people of the rainforest lose their culture and homes. Eight percent of the rainforest is gone and more is on its way to vanishing forever.

Conclusion 2
Animal testing must be stopped. Both humans and animals will benefit greatly if laws are made to abolish this inhumane action. Many steps need to be taken to stop animal testing. By becoming involved and changing your buying habits, we all can be one step closer to the goal of ending animal testing.

Exercise 2
I enjoy sitting on the grass under the tall trees, just as I used to when I was a child.

Exercise 3
Relief means different things to different people. A person that has a test today and isn't ready for it will feel relief when he hears the class will be canceled for today. A person in a marathon will feel relief when he finally crosses the finish line. Relief is a good emotion because it signals you have accomplished something. Carrying a rock up a steep hill says I have done my job. Having a healthy baby says I have done all the right things. Finishing a marathon says I have strength because I crossed the finish line. Relief says you have got the job done.

Unit 12   Summary

Exercise 1
Suggested Answers

Paragraph 1

General

There are several causes of childhood neurosis.

Specific

Four causes of childhood neurosis are "special vulnerabilities", unusual placement in the family "a series of events", or "a series of coincidences".

Paragraph 2

Clearly, in all cases, competence is what's important, but some students would substitute certification for "real competence".

Paragraph 3

When the "torture and violence" of executions are someday "unmasked", out of shame, we will "abolish the death penalty in the United States".

Paragraph 4

"Those few individual inventors who do make it big... are all the more exceptional for being successful entrepreneurs and industrialists as well as inventors".

Paragraph 5

Unlike holidays of the past which were "typically days of actual common celebration", today, like the vacation, "even solemn public holidays... are seen as simply more private leisure time".

Paragraph 6

"There are many new terms and usages that seemed picky or unnecessary to conservatives when they first appeared, but now are indispensable".

Exercise 2

The ability to argue is valuable because we use it for so many reasons: both to make choices for ourselves and to persuade others. Without this ability to argue we lose our power to affect change (Hall & Birkerts, 1998).

Exercise 3

The author advises people who want to stop violence to look at the violence outside and inside themselves without judging, without justifying or condemning it.

Exercise 4

Through analogy, Cleanthes argues that a deity comparable to human intellect exists (Hume, 1990).

Exercise 5

In "No Compassion for Drunk Drivers," Roger Simon explains the anger he felt over viewing a television documentary entitled "Drunk Driving: The Toll, The Tears." He felt enraged by the attitudes expressed both the journalist who produced the documentary, Kelly Burke, and the host of the documentary, Phil Donahue. The source of his anger seemed to grow out of the hypocrisy surrounding this issue that Simon believes exists both in the judicial system and the media. First, Simon uses statistics to point out that drunk driving is a common crime in the United States, and because of that fact, judges and jurors alike are likely to be biased in favor of the drunk driver, he reasons. Secondly, Simon uses a detailed analysis of the images and language in the documentary to illustrate his contention that the media is biased in favor of the drunk driver. His evidence takes the form of language that unquestioningly portrayed the drunk driver as a victim, rather than a criminal. Simon recognizes that his solution to this hypocrisy is unrealistic: a wish that drunk drivers would only kill and maim each other.

Unit 13 How to paraphrase?

Exercise 1

1. *He was good at English.*
2. *He is not satisfied with his present salary.*
3. *She has a good understanding of modern art.*
4. *It is better to prevent it from happening than try to put it right afterwards.*
5. *The teacher told Bob not to be late again.*
6. *They went to swim despite the heavy rain.*
7. *I found this book very difficult to read.*
8. *No once lacked coal that winter.*
9. *Tom likes sports.*
10. *I can no longer tolerate his laziness.*
11. *If you work hard, you will make progress.*
12. *If they hadn't helped us, we wouldn't have succeeded.*
13. *There are a number of books for you to choose.*
14. *I was serious about it. I plan to work hard next term and I mean it.*
15. *He had waited for her for a long time, but she didn't come. He wanted to leave.*
16. *We all waited for you last night because we thought you would come to the party.*

Exercise 2

1. The little girl sat on the floor surrounded by toys.
2. The book contained information about modern science.
3. In the evenings, he engaged in his hobbies.
4. Helicopters, unlike other forms of transport, do not need ground installations to operate.

5. The man was in a great hurry that morning.

Exercise 3
1. People trying to interpret a situation often base their reactions on those around them.
2. Three things are necessary for bystanders to intervene in an emergency.
3. In a crowd, then, each person tends to notice a potential emergency less than when alone.
4. Even if a person decides that an event is an emergency...
5. ... each person may feel less inclined to intervene in the presence of other bystanders.

Exercise 4

A paraphrase:
In research papers students often quote excessively, failing to keep quoted material down to a desirable level. Since the problem usually originates during note taking, it is essential to minimize the material recorded verbatim (Lester 46-47).

A summary:
Students should take just a few notes in direct quotation from sources to help minimize the amount of quoted material in a research paper (Lester 46-47).

Exercise 5
1. According to Jacques Cousteau, the activity of people in Antarctica is jeopardizing a delicate natural mechanism that controls the earth's climate. He fears that human activity could interfere with the balance between the sun, the source of the earth's heat, and the important source of cold from Antarctic waters that flow north and cool the oceans and atmosphere ("Captain Cousteau" 17).
2. During the twenties lawlessness and social nonconformity prevailed. In cities organized crime flourished without police interference, and in spite of nationwide prohibition of liquor sales, anyone who wished to buy a drink knew where to get one. Musicians like Louis Armstrong become favorites, particularly among young people, as many turned away from highly respectable classical music to jazz. One of the best examples of the anti-traditional trend was the proliferation of young "flappers", women who rebelled against custom by cutting off their hair and shortening their skirts (Yancey 25).
3. The use of a helmet is the key to reducing bicycling fatalities, which are due to head injuries 75% of the time. By cushioning the head upon impact, a helmet can reduce accidental injury by as much as 85%, saving the lives of hundreds of victims annually, half of whom are school children ("Bike Helmets" 348).
4. Matisse paintings are remarkable in giving the viewer the distinct sensory impressions of one experiencing the scene first hand. For instance, "The Casbah Gate" takes one to the walled city of Tangier and the Bab el Aassa gateway near the Sultan's palace, where one can imagine standing on an afternoon, absorbing the splash of colors and the fine

outlines. Even the sentry, the bowaab vaguely eyeing those who come and go through the gate, blends into the scene as though real (Plagens 50).
5. How much higher skyscrapers of the future will rise than the present world marvel, the Sears Tower, is unknown. However, the design of one twice as tall is already on the boards, and an architect, Robert Sobel, thinks we currently have sufficient know-how to build a skyscraper with over 500 stories (Bachman 15).

<h1 style="text-align:center">Unit 14   Framing your voice in argumentation</h1>

Exercise 1
Individual and Appropriate Voice

Everyone's writing needs to be different from everyone else's. And the only way that happens is if writers make different choices when they write, choices about the topics they pick, the words they use, the details they include, different beginning and ending strategies, and so on. The set of all the different choices a writer's makes determines, and the collective effect they have on the reader, is what is often called the "voice" in a piece of writing. Voice, sometimes referred to as "tone" or "mood" or even "style", tells the reader about the writer's personality in the piece.

The Writer Cares About the Topic

Does the writer of *Chores* care about her topic? I think she does. First of all, she has chosen a topic from her life, something that she has to deal with on a regular basis. Most of us care about what happens to us in our own lives and that's why writing about one's life is probably the most common type of topic writer's choose. The second thing I notice is a very strong opinion. There's no doubt about how this writer feels about doing chores. The third thing that tells me this writer cares about her topic is all the detail she includes to support her opinion. If she didn't care about doing chores, she probably wouldn't have very much to say about it, and what she did say probably wouldn't be very detailed. But throughout this piece, over and over, this writer is telling us how chores affect her life and how she feels about that.

Strong Feelings, Honest Statements

The writer of *Chores* certainly has no problem communicating her strong feelings. The piece is packed with emotion in almost every sentence. But are those feelings honest? Does the piece sound genuine, as though the writer really believes what she's saying? Of course, there's no way to tell for sure. She could have made the whole thing up. So because we can't question the writer, we have to question the writing.

Individual, Authentic, and Original

In *Chores*, I sense the writer's individuality very clearly. Though I know that many kids her age complain about having to do chores, the way she's complaining about it strikes me as unique. She has such well-defined and detailed opinions that I can't imagine another kid expressing these exact feelings in exactly the same way. I think *Chores* shows a lot of individuality and that's another important reason why it's such a successful piece.

To me, *Chores* seems very authentic. It sounds like it was written by a frustrated 9-year-old girl who doesn't like to do her chores; the writer's voice matches is consistent throughout and matches my expectation of how I think this person should sound.

Chores feels very original to me. I've never seen a piece on this topic that sounds quite the same. Of course, to someone who had read 20 other pieces just like it, it wouldn't seem that way.

Displays a Definite and Well Developed Personality

In *Chores*, I feel like I'm getting to know a frustrated little girl who has a pretty good sense of humor and, deep down, a reasonable attitude about doing her chores. She doesn't like to do chores, but she also knows they're a part of life we all just have to get through. To me, her personality in this piece seems well defined and successfully developed.

Appropriate Tone for Purpose and Audience

I think the voice the writer uses in *Chores* matches the situation very well.

Exercise 2

Humorous and ironical. The writer is actually telling the readers what kind of argument is ineffective.

Unit 15 How to synthesizing information

Suggested answer:

Water is the most common substance on earth (Crystal, 1990, p. 1285). In the form of seas and oceans, it covers approximately three quarters of the earth's surface. It is necessary for our present way of life as without it we cannot live.

However, in almost every country of the world, there is a water problem. This problem is the lack of suitable water. The two main reasons for this lack is the scarcity of fresh water resources and pollution of the small amount of water that we have. Most of the water on the planet is saltwater, which humans cannot make use of ("Water: The facts," 2003), and, of the small amount of freshwater available only 0.01% is usable. The water is also unevenly distributed so it is not always available where it is needed. Furthermore, this small amount of water needs to support a growing world population, which needs more food and industrial products. Both food and industrial products need water for their production.

A further problem, though, is the pollution of these scarce natural resources. Some pollution is natural and this is difficult to prevent. However Barnes-Svarney (1996, p. 742) stresses that much pollution is caused by the activities of humans. Industrial processes contaminate the water with poisons and bacteria and private houses pollute the water with sewage.

It is essential therefore that this problem is addressed very soon. New ways to obtain water from the earth need to be found; human beings need to reduce the amount of water that they use as well as ensuring that the small supply of water that is available is not polluted so it is available for use.

References

Barnes-Svarney, P. (1996). *The New York public library science desk reference.* New York: Macmillan.

Crystal, D. (1990). *The Cambridge encyclopaedia.* Cambridge: Cambridge University Press.

Water: The facts. (2003). *New Internationalist*, 354, 18.

Unit 16　Reporting verbs

Exercise 1

1m, 2f, 3c, 4o, 5l, 6n, 7k, 8d, 9b, 10h, 11e, 12g, 13a, 14p, 15i, 16j

Exercise 2

1B, 2F, 3C, 4E, 5A, 6D

Exercise 3

1c, 2f, 3a, 4b, 5d, 6e

Exercise 4

would arrive

shouldn't smoke

was crying

had left

were not married

Exercise 5

1. denied
2. invited
3. suggested
4. promised
5. hoped
6. begged
7. refused
8. advised
9. insisted
10. reminded
11. threatened
12. warned

Exercise 6

1. explained
2. promised
3. apologized
4. offered
5. admitted
6. added
7. protested
8. begged

Unit 17　Argument

Exercise 1

　　In this argument prudent investors are advised to stop investing in hotels and invest instead in hospitals and nursing homes. The author cites two related trends — an aging population and a decline in hotel occupancy — as grounds for this advice. To illustrate these trends, the author refers to another region of the country, where 20 percent of the population is over 65 years old and where occupancy rates in resort hotels have declined significantly during the past six months. This argument is unconvincing in a couple of important respects.

　　In the first place, the author provides no evidence to support the claim that the population as a whole is aging and that the hotel occupancy rate in general is declining. The example cited, while suggestive of these trends, is insufficient to warrant their truth because there is no reason to believe that data drawn from this unnamed region is representative of the entire country. For example, if the region from which the data was gathered was Florida, it would clearly be unrepresentative. The reason for this is obvious. Florida is populated by a disproportionate number of retired people over 65 years old and is a very popular vacation destination during the winter months. Moreover, resort hotel occupancy in Florida typically declines significantly during the summer months.

　　In the second place, the author has provided no evidence to support the claim that the decline in hotel occupancy is related to the aging of the population. The author appears to believe that the decrease in occupancy rates at resort hotels is somehow caused by the increase in the number of people over age 65. However, the example cited by the author establishes only that these two trends are correlated; it does not establish that the decline in hotel occupancy is due to an increase in the number of people over the age of 65.

　　In conclusion, the author's investment advice is not based on sound reasoning. To strengthen the conclusion, the author must show that the trends were not restricted to a particular region of the country. The author must also show that the cause of the decline in hotel occupancy is the increase in the number of people over 65.

Exercise 2

Citing facts drawn from the color-film processing industry that indicate a downward trend in the costs of film processing over a 24-year period, the author argues that Olympic Foods will likewise be able to minimize costs and thus maximize profits in the future. In support of this conclusion the author cites the general principle that "as organizations learn how to do things better, they become more efficient." This principle, coupled with the fact that Olympic Foods has had 25 years of experience in the food processing industry leads to the author's rosy prediction. This argument is unconvincing because it suffers from two critical flaws.

First, the author's forecast of minimal costs and maximum profits rests on the gratuitous assumption that Olympic Foods' "long experience" has taught it how to do things better. There is, however, no guarantee that this is the case. Nor does the author cite any evidence to support this assumption. Just as likely, Olympic Foods has learned nothing from its 25 years in the food-processing business. Lacking this assumption, the expectation of increased efficiency is entirely unfounded.

Second, it is highly doubtful that the facts drawn from the color-film processing industry are applicable to the food processing industry. Differences between the two industries clearly outweigh the similarities, thus making the analogy highly less than valid. For example, problems of spoilage, contamination, and timely transportation all affect the food industry but are virtually absent in the film processing industry. Problems such as these might present insurmountable obstacles that prevent lowering food-processing costs in the future.

As it stands the author's argument is not compelling, to strengthen the conclusion that Olympic Foods will enjoy minimal costs and maximum profits in the future, the author would have to provide evidence that the company has learned how to do things better as a result of its 25 years of experience. Supporting examples drawn from industries more similar to the food-processing industry would further substantiate the author's view.

Exercise 3

Sample 1

In this argument, the author indicates that it is cost-effective to replace real flowers by artificial flowers. To support his conclusion, the author points out that those real flowers need more water to survive in mid-summer. In addition, he reasons that even though the use of artificial flowers spends twice the amount of money of the maintenance of real flowers initially, people will be beneficial to this alternative in a long run. Moreover, a recent survey quoted is cited citizens' dissatisfaction with the fiscal performance and their hope of reduction of public spending. As I analyze this argument in close concert, the author's view is not very convincing for three major reasons.

In the first place, the evidence the author provides is insufficient to support that the use of artificial flowers can reduce public spending, even in a long run. The author may emphasize the merit of artificial flowers that they never need water to survive or grow. But he fails to notice that over time, the outside artificial flowers inevitably become messy and dirty, weakening their decorative function. Then people also have to wash them with considerable amount of water. Furthermore, the sun fades the color of artificial flowers. Hence, the city need spend a supplementary cost to replace old ones.

In the second place, the author distorts the readers' ideas about ways to reduce public spending. Readers never specify that an end to the use of real flowers should be one way to reduce public expense. Readers may call for changes in other public work and services other than the replacement of real flowers. As far as I know, lots of people have inherent preferences for real flowers, due to their peculiar features. When real flowers are blossoming, fragrant smell spreads over a large area. Compared with artificial flowers, real flowers can change their appearance at all seasons.

In the third place, the survey quoted by the author is worthless because some of its details have not been provided. Without additional information, such as the total number of people in the city or the framework of who were conducted, the result of the survey may lack representative. We can picture that the city has a population of more than 5 million, but this survey conducted only 1 200 people, especially readers who are easily affected by the gazette's editorial.

Since the author commits logical mistakes mentioned above and fails to consider the whole situation comprehensively, his ideas should not be adopted. The conclusion would be strengthened if he can obviate these three major logical mistakes.

Sample 2

In this argument, the author makes a conclusion that the city should plant artificial flowers instead of real flowers in big decorative pot on Main Street. The author's line of reasoning is established on his assumption that by planting plastic flowers, the city can save money. To support such an assumption, the author cites three supportive examples: last year, the city contracted with Flower Power to plant a variety of flowers and to water them each, yet by midsummer many of the plants were wilted; although the initial cost for plastic flowers is twice as much as real plants, the city can save money after two years; finally, public reaction will definitely support the proposal. At the first glance, the argument seems to be somewhat convincing. However, a close and deep reflection reveals how groundless and problematic it is. In the following paragraphs, I should elaborate the main flaws in the argument.

In the first place, the author fails to explore the real underlying reasons for the death of the plants and flowers. Instead, he makes a gratuitous assumption that more frequent watering is needed. However, the author fails to substantiate his point. In no case can the mere fact that the flowers are wilted help to build up such an assumption flawlessly. It is possible that many of the plants were wilted because they required drier soils for survival and thriving. Unless the author can build up a causal correlation between the survival of the plants and more needed watering, the assumption remains questionable and open to discussion.

In the second place, the author mentions that planting plastic flowers means the saving of money in the long run. However, the credibility of such an assertion has yet to be established, especially since the author ignores to point out that most of the plastic plants will last for more than two years. One obvious rebuttal to the author's reasoning is that investigations show that a majority of plastic plants, if planted on the Main Street, can only last for at most two years without the protection from direct sunshine. In such a case, the author's assertion that planting plastic plants will save money is of dubious validity.

In the third place, the author believes that the public will certainly support his position, as over 1 200 Gazette readers said that the city wastes money and should find ways to reduce spending. Yet, such a survey result is neither representative nor reliable. Actually, it is rather misleading, since the author lacks direct evidence to buoy his assumption that the viewpoint of the 1 200 Gazette can largely reflects the opinion of the majority of the residents. Besides, even if most of the residents do favor for a reduced spending, they may not necessarily consider the author's suggestion a proper way of reduction in expenditure. Therefore, the author makes a hasty conclusion that the public will support his position for sure.

To sum up, because it is plagued with the above-stated fallacies, the argument is flawed. To buttress his argument, the author should provide more direct evidence indicating that planting plastic plants will be more money-saving than planting real flowers. Moreover, the feasibility of planting and maintaining the plastic plants should also be taken into consideration. Additionally, a more related and reliable survey showing the real support for the author's recommendation will also cement the author's position.

Unit 18 Reference

Exercise 1

	Author	Title of book	Place of publication	Publisher	Date
e.g.	J. C. Alderson	Assessing reading	Cambridge	Cambridge University Press	2001
1	American Psychological Association	Publication manual of the American Psychological Association	Washington, D C	American Psychological Association	2001
2	C. Bazerman	Shaping written knowledge	Madison, W I	University of Wisconsin Press	1989
3	J. Bell	Doing your research project	Buckingham	Open University Press	1999
4	S. Benesch	Critical English for academic purposes	Malwah, N J	Lawrence Erlbaum Associates	2001

	Author	Title of book	Place of publication	Publisher	Date
5	T. Bex	Variety in written English	London	Routledge	1996
6	A. J. Herbert	The structure of technical English	London	Longman	1965
7	T. M. Lillis	Student writing: Access, regulation, desire	London	Routledge	2001
8	M. McCarthy & R. Carter	Language as discourse	London	Longman	1994
9	P. Ramsden	Learning to teach in higher education	London	Routledge	1992
10	J. Swales	Other floors, other voices	Mahwah, N J	Lawrence Erlbaum	1998

Exercise 2

	Author	Title of article	Title of journal	Journal volume	Page numbers	Date
e. g.	E. Abo Mosallem	English for police officers in Egypt	English for Specific Purposes	3	171-182	1984
1	B. L. Bayne	Some effects of stress in the adult on the larval development of Mytilus edulis	Nature	237	459-475	1972
2	T. Becher	Towards a definition of disciplinary cultures	Studies in Higher Education	6	109-122	1981
3	D. Belcher	How professors initiate non-native speakers into their disciplinary discourse communities	Texas Papers in Foreign Language Education	1	207-225	1989
4	T. G. Cummings	Self-regulating work groups: A socio-technical synthesis	Academy of Management Review	3	625-634	1978
5	J. Fitzgerald	The misconceived revolution: State and society in China's nationalist revolution, 1923-1926	Journal of Asian Studies	49	323-343	1990
6	D. C. Hallin	Sound Bite News: Television Coverage of Elections, 1968-1988	Journal of Communication	42	5-24	1992
7	S. Harris. & P. Ghauri.	Strategy formation by business leaders: Exploring the influence of national values	European Journal of Marketing	34	126-142	2000

	Author	Title of article	Title of journal	Journal volume	Page numbers	Date
8	K. Hyltenstam	Implicational patterns in interlanguage syntax variation	Language Learning	27	383-411	1977
9	J. A. A. Sillince	Extending the cognitive approach to strategic change in organizations: Some theory	British Journal of Management	6	59-76	1995
10	B. W. Tuckman	Developmental sequences in small groups	Psychological Bulletin	63	384-399	1965

Exercise 3

Books: 2, 7, 8, 10, 12
Journals: 1, 3, 4, 5, 6, 9, 11, 13

Exercise 4

1. Alderson, J. C., Krahnke, K. J. & Standfield, C. W. (Eds.). (1987). *Reviews of English language proficiency tests*. Washington, D C: TESOL.
2. Carol, B. J. & West, R. (1989). *ESU framework: Performance scales for English language examinations*. London: Longman.
3. Chafe, W. (1982). Integration and involvement in speaking, writing, and oral literature. In D. Tannen (Ed.), *Spoken and written language: Exploring orality and literacy* (pp. 35-53). Norwood, N J: Ablex Publishing Corporation.
4. Cookson, L. (1984). *Writing*. London: Hutchinson.
5. Davies, A., & Criper, C. (1987). *Research report 1: ELTS validation project report*. Edinburgh: University of Edinburgh.
6. Davies, E. & Whitney, N. (1981). *Strategies for reading*. London: Heinemann.
7. Davies, S. & West, R. (1984). *The Pitman Guide To English Language Examinations* (2nd ed.). London: Pitman.
8. Ferguson, N. & O'Reilly, M. (1977). *Listening and note taking*. London: Evans.
9. Hogue, A. (1996). *First steps in academic writing*. London: Longman.
10. International English Language Testing System (1989). *An Introduction to IELTS*. London: The British Council.
11. Jones, L. (1981). *Functions of English*. Cambridge: Cambridge University Press.
12. Laird, E. (1977). *English in focus: English in education*. Oxford: Oxford University Press.
13. Murphy, R. (1985). *English grammar in use*. Oxford: Oxford University Press.
14. Northedge, A. (1990). *The good study guide*. Milton Keynes: The Open University Press.

15. O'Connor, J. D. (1980). *Better English pronunciation* (new ed.). Cambridge: Cambridge University Press.
16. Pirie, D. B. (1985). *How to write critical essays*. London: Routledge.
17. Walker, T. (1992). *English for academic purposes-computer science*. London: Prentice Hall.
18. Wong, R., Glendinning, E. & Mantell, H. (1994). *Becoming a writer*. London: Longman.
19. Yates, C. St. J. (1992). *English for academic purposes-Agriculture*. London: Prentice Hall.
20. Zimmerman, F. (1989). *English for science*. London: Prentice Hall.

Bibliography

1. Bailey, S. *Academic Writing: A Practical Guide for Students* [M]. London: RoutledgeFalmer. 2004.
2. Bander, Robert G. *American English Rhetoric: A Writing Program in English as a Second Language* [M]. New York: Holt, Rinehart and Winston. 1983.
3. Bell, Judith, *Doing Your Research Project* [M]. Open University Press. 1993.
4. Fairbairn, Gavin J and Christopher Winch. *Reading, Writing and Reasoning: A Guide for Students* [M]. 2nd ed. Buckingham: Open University Press. 1996.
5. Hamp-Lyons, L. Heasley, B. *Study Writing* [M]. Cambridge University Press. 2006.
6. Hennesey, Brendan. *Writing an Essay: Simple Techniques to Transform your Coursework and Examinations* [M]. Oxford: Howtobooks. 2004.
7. Jordan, R R. *Academic Writing Course* [M]. London: Longman. 1999.
8. Kane, Thomas S. *The New Oxford Guide to Writing* [M]. New York: Oxford University Press. 1994.
9. Lester, James D. *Writing Research Paper. A Complete Guide* [M]. 9th ed. New York: Longman. 1999.
10. Levin, Peter. *Write Great Essays!: Reading and Essay Writing for Undergraduates and Taught Postgraduates* [M]. Maidenhead: Oxford University Press. 2004.
11. Mounsey, Chris. *Essays and Dissertations* [M]. Oxford: Oxford University Press. 2002.
12. Oshima and Hogue. *Writing Academic English* [M]. Longman. 2006.
13. Oshima, A. & Hogue, A. *Writing Academic English* [M]. 2nd ed. California: Addison Wesley. 1991.
14. Redman, Peter. *Good Essay Writing* [M]. London: Sage publications. 2001.
15. Slade, Carole. *Form and Style: Research Papers, Reports and Theses* 如何写研究论文和学术报告 [M]. 外语教学与研究出版社. 2000.
16. Smith, Pauline. *Writing an Assignment: Effective Ways to Improve Your Research and Presentation Skills* [M]. Oxford: How to Books Ltd.. 2002.
17. Soles, Derek. *The Academic Essay: How to Plan, Draft, Write and Revise* [M]. Bishops Lydeared: Studymates. 2005.
18. Stott, Rebecca, et al. *Making Your Case: A Practical Guide to Essay Writing* [M]. Harlow: Longman. 2001
19. Swales, J. *Genre analysis: English in academic and research settings* [M]. Cambridge. 1990.
20. Swales, J. M. and Feak, C. B. *Academic Writing for Graduate Students* [M]. Ann Arbor: University of Michigan Press. 1994.
21. Swan, Michael. *Practical English Usage* [M]. 2nd ed. Oxford: Oxford University Press. 1995.

22. Teitelbaum, H. *How to Write a Thesis*[M]. 上海译文出版社. 2005.
23. Truss, Lynne. *Eats, Shoots & Leaves: the Zero Tolerance Approach to Punctuation*[M]. London: profile Books. 2003.
24. Wallace, Michael J, *Study Skills in English*[M]. Cambridge: Cambridge University Press. 2004.
25. Walliman. Nicholas. *Your Undergraduate Dissertations: The Essential Guide for Success*[M]. London: Sage Publications. 2004.
26. Wyse, Dominic. *The Good Writing Guide for Education Students*[M]. London: Sage Publications. 2006.
27. 程爱民,祁寿华. 英语学术论文写作纲要[M]. 上海:上海外语教育出版社,2005.
28. 冯幼明. 高级英文写作教程:论文写作[M]. 北京:北京大学出版社,2002.
29. 黄国文,葛达西,张美芳. 英语学术论文写作[M]. 重庆:重庆大学出版社,2004.
30. 林奈尔. 大学英文写作[M]. 南京:南京大学出版社,1997.
31. 刘洊波. 英语学术论文写作[M]. 北京:高等教育出版社,2004.
32. 刘新民. 英语论文写作规范[M]. 北京:高等教育出版社,2003.
33. 祁寿华. 西方写作理论、教学与实践[M]. 上海:上海外语教育出版社,2000.
34. 李旭. 英语科技论文写作指南[M]. 北京:国防工业出版社,2005.
35. 毛荣贵. 英语写作纵横谈[M]. 上海:上海外语教育出版社,1997.
36. 范家材. 英语修辞赏析[M]. 上海:上海交通大学出版社,1992.
37. 郭秀梅. 实用英语修辞学[M]. 南京:江苏人民出版社,1984.
38. 刘洊波,李如平. 大学英语论文写作手册[M]. 重庆:重庆大学出版社,1999.
39. 穆诗雄. 英语专业毕业论文写作[M]. 北京:外语教学与研究出版社,2002.
40. 祁寿华. 高级英语写作指南[M]. 上海:上海外语教育出版社,2001.
41. 石坚,帅培天. 英语论文写作[M]. 成都:四川人民出版社,2005.
42. 覃先美,等. 毕业论文导写[M]. 长沙:湖南师范大学出版社,2001.
43. 文秋芳. 应用语言学研究方法与论文写作[M]. 北京:外语教学与研究出版社,2004.